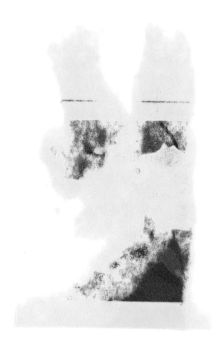

Southern Literary Studies
Louis D. Rubin, Jr., Editor

Porch Talk with Ernest Gaines

Porch Talk
with
Ernest Gaines

Conversations on the Writer's Craft

MARCIA GAUDET
and
CARL WOOTON

LOUISIANA STATE UNIVERSITY PRESS

BATON ROUGE and LONDON

Copyright © 1990 by Louisiana State University Press
All rights reserved
Manufactured in the United States of America
First printing
99 98 97 96 95 94 93 92 91 90   5 4 3 2 1

Designer: Amanda McDonald Key
Typeface: Sabon
Typesetter: G & S Typesetters, Inc.
Printer and binder: Thomson-Shore, Inc.

Library of Congress Cataloging-in-Publication Data

Gaudet, Marcia G.
  Porch talk with Ernest Gaines : conversations on the writer's
craft / Marcia Gaudet and Carl Wooton.
    p.   cm.
  ISBN 0-8071-1589-4 (alk. paper)
  1. Gaines, Ernest J., 1933–   —Interviews. 2. Novelists,
American—20th century—Interviews. 3. Fiction—Authorship.
I. Gaines, Ernest J., 1933–   . II. Wooton, Carl, 1934–   .
III. Title.
PS3557.A355Z68   1990
813'.54—dc20   90-31985
                                                        CIP

The authors are grateful to the editors and publishers of the following publications for
permission to reprint material that originally appeared in a different form under the
following titles: "Talking with Ernest J. Gaines," *Callaloo* (Summer, 1988), 229–43,
published by the Johns Hopkins University Press; "Ernest J. Gaines," *The Best of
Lafayette* (November–December, 1986), 32–37.
  Material from "An Interview with Ernest J. Gaines," conducted by Carl Wooton and
Marcia Gaudet, *New Orleans Review*, Vol. 14, no. 4, copyright © 1987 by Loyola
University, New Orleans, is reprinted by permission of the *New Orleans Review*.

Frontispiece is reproduced courtesy USL News Service, photograph by Doug Dugas.

In summer, they would sit out on the porch, the gallery—"the garry," we called it—and they would talk for hours. . . . I did not know then that twenty or twenty-five years later I would try to put some of their talk in a book which I would title *The Autobiography of Miss Jane Pittman.*

—Ernest Gaines

Contents

Illustrations

Porch Talk with Ernest Gaines

Introduction

Ernest J. Gaines has created an array of characters and conflicts as rich
in their variety and in their universality as any in American literature.
Gaines's characters evoke laughter, joy, despair, grief, anger, sympa-
thy, and—perhaps most of all—pride. Whatever their struggles, their
successes and failures, they move toward a perception of their dignity.
That perception often comes at a high price: at the cost of love, freedom, or life. In a single act or from a fragment of dialogue, his characters discover the difference between the anonymity of a stereotype
and the individuality that comes only when one grasps his manhood.
It does not matter to Gaines at what age that process happens. It is
equally significant in the eight-year-old James in "The Sky Is Gray"
and in the men of seventy and eighty who discover courage and the
sustaining strength of community in *A Gathering of Old Men.*

Gaines was born on January 15, 1933, in Oscar, a small town in
Pointe Coupée Parish, Louisiana. The center of his world as he grew
up was the old slave quarters on River Lake Plantation, where five
generations of his family have lived. Gaines's parents separated when
he was eight years old, and he recalls being raised chiefly by an aunt,
Augustine Jefferson. He credits her with having taught him the importance of sacrifice and work, of integrity and courage, and of doing all
things with dignity. His early schooling consisted of six years at the
elementary school in the one-room church in the quarters and three
years at St. Augustine, a Catholic school for blacks in New Roads, the
parish seat of Pointe Coupée Parish. Immediately after World War II,
Gaines's mother moved to California to be with his stepfather. Gaines
remained in Louisiana to do the labor around the house that his aunt,
who was crippled, could not do. He also was responsible for two
younger brothers and a sister. In 1948, because there was no high

school for black students in Pointe Coupée Parish, he joined his mother and stepfather in Vallejo, California. He graduated from high school there, served in the army in the early fifties, returned to California, and graduated from San Francisco State College in 1957. He won a creative writing fellowship to attend Stanford University in 1958–1959. His classmates there included Wendell Berry and Ken Kesey.

Growing up in the quarters, Gaines was part of an oral culture that was rural, black, and bilingual (English and French). The setting for all his works is the general area of South Louisiana where he grew up. The fictional town of Bayonne is based on New Roads. Although Gaines has lived in San Francisco most of his adult life, he has maintained close contact with the place where he grew up and with the people who have remained there. He reveals in his conversations with us a deep concern for the land of this small area, for the cemetery where the dead are buried, and for the lives of the old people who tend small gardens in summer and, in winter, gather around fireplaces in wooden frame houses that are more than a hundred years old. Although none of Gaines's fiction is autobiographical, there is always the strong influence of culture and family in his works.

His first novel, *Catherine Carmier*, appeared in 1964. Jackson Guerin is a young black man who returns for a visit to the quarters after having been away for several years. He has an education, and some of the older women in the quarters expect him to stay and teach the children. Jackson has no intention of staying. He falls in love with Catherine, the light-skinned daughter of Raoul Carmier. The conflict develops along two lines that recur in later works: between Raoul, who is light-skinned and without a son, and Jackson, who is dark-skinned and without a father. In *Of Love and Dust* (1967), Gaines produced a fast-paced narrative about Marcus, a young black man who, as an alternative to prison, accepts being bonded into virtual servitude to a white plantation owner. Marcus is another young man without a father and without a place in the world. Angry and bitter, he eventually seeks revenge for the petty cruelties of a white overseer by seducing the man's wife. The narrator, Jim Kelly, is older and much mellower than Marcus. He presents himself as a detached observer, similar to his own perception of God as an old man playing solitaire after having decided that humankind has turned out to be not worth much attention.

Bloodline, a collection of five stories, was published in 1968. Gaines claims that the stories were arranged in an effort to create an effect similar to that of William Faulkner's *Go Down, Moses*. The time frames of the stories range from the early forties to the period of civil rights conflicts in the sixties. Each set of central characters is older from the first story to the last, and the conflicts become more complex and intense. These stories exhibit the range of Gaines's vision and talents, from the comedy of "A Long Day in November" to the tragic madness of the mulatto Copper in the title story. There are, also, the thematic movement toward manhood in "The Sky Is Gray" and the devastating effects of abandonment by the father in "Three Men" and "Bloodline." In "Just Like a Tree," Aunt Fe prefigures the courage and determination of the old men in *A Gathering of Old Men*. A children's book, *A Long Day in November* (1971), is a revised version of the short story of the same name.

Probably the best known of Gaines's novels is *The Autobiography of Miss Jane Pittman* (1971). Gaines has called the book a "folk autobiography." It is the fictional retelling of the life story of a 107-year-old black woman. Miss Jane recounts a hundred years of a life that included a childhood in slavery, love and marriage to a strong man, the effects of his death, the murder of a schoolteacher because he was critical of white society, and the hardships of finding a place in a world structured to deny her one. After Gaines told Miss Jane's story, he worked for seven years on *In My Father's House* (1978), which he has called the novel he had to write and the only one he was never able to finish the way he wanted it to be. It is a tragic story of a son's search for recognition from his father and the father's own search for the courage and integrity to admit his paternity. It also explores Gaines's vision of the dilemma of the civil rights leader of the sixties, the man dedicated to a good cause who finds that the intensity of his dedication can diminish his humanity. It is the darkest of Gaines's works, the only one unrelieved by humor.

Gaines's most recent published work, *A Gathering of Old Men*, came out in 1983. It is set in quarters similar to those found in the other works, but the action occurs in the late seventies. Gaines presents a variety of first-person narrators, most of them old men who have decided, for the first time in their lives, to stand against the threat of violence from white men. Each of the old men gets a chance to reveal the pain he has accumulated and borne over seventy years or more. Each reveals the ultimate humiliation of having to accede to a world that denies him his manhood. In this novel the different voices present a vision of human character in which the comic elements are essential ingredients of integrity and dignity.

In 1981 the Department of English at the University of Southwestern Louisiana had the opportunity to invite Gaines to be a visiting professor. The relationship that developed between Gaines and the faculty—as well as the obvious value he had as a teacher of creative writing—led the university to offer him a permanent position as writer-in-residence. He has held that position since 1983. He lives in Lafayette through the academic year, but he retreats annually to San Francisco to escape the Louisiana summer heat.

Through our association with him we have discovered that dignity and pride are not only themes that pervade his art, but qualities that characterize him as a teacher and as a man. We came to do these interviews because we discovered in our conversations with each other (and with Ernest Gaines, during the years when all three of us were members of the English faculty at USL) that our separate areas of interest were complementary. Both of us teach American literature and practice formal literary criticism, but one (Marcia Gaudet) has a primary interest in folklore and the other (Carl Wooton) has a primary interest in writing fiction.

The role of folklore in black literature has been widely recognized. Houston A. Baker, Jr., has said, "At the foundation of the black American literary tradition stands black folklore."[1] Gaines frequently has remarked on his own work in ways that suggest a richness of texture for the folklorist to explore. He understands and values the oral culture in which he grew up, but he does not accept that culture

1. Houston A. Baker, Jr., *Long Black Song: Essays in Black American Literature and Culture* (Charlottesville, 1972), 18.

or its traditions unquestioningly. As Keith Byerman has pointed out, Gaines's fiction is firmly rooted in the folk culture and recognizes that culture's values, but it also recognizes "that the folk community itself . . . can become an imprisoning force."[2]

The questions that rose out of the importance of folk culture and folk idiom led into the discussions we had about narrative technique and point of view. Gaines reveals how his ability to capture the essential quality of the voices of his people, what he calls "the sound of my people talking," comes from his technical training and broad literary background. Though he bases his narrative form on the folk story-telling tradition, he is quite obviously not a folk storyteller. He is an artist who recognizes the value of the language and customs of his culture, and who consciously manipulates that material through techniques and in forms that occupy the mainstream of Western literary tradition.

The primary focus of these interviews, which were conducted between October of 1986 and May of 1987, is on the body of work produced by Ernest J. Gaines. Those who have read Gaines's fiction know the importance of the image of people sitting on porches and talking to one another about what they see and hear up and down the road that runs through the quarters. That image, combined with Gaines's conversations with us on the sun porch of his residence in Lafayette, provided us with our title. These conversations explore both Gaines's development as a writer and the process of transforming folk narrative and culture into literature.

2. Keith Byerman, *Fingering the Jagged Grain: Tradition and Form in Recent Black Fiction* (Athens, Ga., 1985), 67.

1

Oral Tradition and Literature

MG: In interviews over the years, you have talked about your work, how you see yourself as a writer, and what you're trying to do with your writing.

GAINES: You'll have to remind me of that.

MG: OK. I've thought to remind you. What I want to see is if you've changed that perspective. One thing that you've said over and over again is that you see yourself as a storyteller and that you came up from a place that was oral, where people talked the stories. In 1969 you said: "I like to listen to the way people talk. I like to listen to their stories. Then when I get into a little room someplace I try to write them down."[1] Then in 1974 you said: "I come from a long line of storytellers. I come from a plantation where people told stories by the fireplace at night. People told stories on the ditch bank. . . . People sat around telling stories. I think in my immediate family there were tremendous storytellers or liars—"

GAINES: Right, right, yes.

MG: "—or whatever you want to call them. They would talk and talk and talk, and I'd listen to them."[2] Again, a few years later—in 1979—you said, "We talked because the old people could not write."[3] In your work you've taken this oral tradition of storytelling and transformed it into literature.

GAINES: Right, I try to do that. That's one of the hardest things in the world to do. You can go to any place, any bar on the corner out

1. Gregory Fitz Gerald and Peter Marchant, "An Interview: Ernest J. Gaines," *New Orleans Review*, I (1969), 333.

2. Ruth Laney, "A Conversation with Ernest Gaines," *Southern Review*, n.s., X (1974), 3.

3. Patricia Rickels, "An Interview with Ernest J. Gaines," *Southwestern Review*, IV (1979), 33.

there, and find people who can tell the greatest stories in the world—they can tell you some stories. But if you give one of them a pen and some paper and say, "OK, write this stuff down," he'll run. He'll drop those things and start running. It's a tough thing to do, to try to recapture these things. But I try to do that, yes.

MG: How do you make that leap from the oral storytelling tradition to the literary medium?

GAINES: Well, I think it's a combination of things. I think Joyce does it. I think he does it in *Finnegans Wake*, and nobody can understand what the hell is going on there. I think he also did it in other stories. I think a good example would be "Ivy Day in the Committee Room." It's the old tradition of these old guys telling the story about the great fighter—the Irish patriot, Parnell—and Joyce can put this in literature because Joyce had such a great literary background. Faulkner does the same thing. "Spotted Horses" is nothing but a guy telling a story about some wild horses beating up on somebody, cutting people up and running people all over the place, and Twain does the same thing. Twain and Faulkner are the fathers of this, this combination of that oral tradition and then integrating it into a literary tradition. So it's something that I inherited from having that kind of background and then having studied literature.

MG: Do you think it's possible for a writer to be able to do this if he's not, first of all, a part of that oral tradition?

GAINES: I think a writer writes about what he is part of. I think he has to. I don't know that he could do it if he does not have this kind of background. I don't know that Faulkner could have written what he wrote if he had not come from that kind of background, where people squatted around the stores or the courthouse square. I don't know if Twain could have done it had he not been part of that traditional Mississippi River storytelling crowd, and then knowing literature. And I don't know if you can do the same thing if you don't have that kind of tradition.

MG: If you try to transcribe oral storytelling literally, what you come out with is flat. To do what you do and what Faulkner does, is to add to the writing something to compensate for not having the audience and the sound and the performance there. You substitute with your writing whatever is missing from the performance.

GAINES: And then you leave off things, too. You leave out some of the things that they do tell you in order to make it in that literary form. You're transferring from the oral thing, a guy sitting there telling you a story. You have to take what he's telling you, and you have to use those twenty-six letters over here to put this thing down accurately. You try to put it down very accurately. But then you know you cannot do it, because you cannot use all the gestures: you cannot use all the sounds of his voice, his improper use of syntax, whatever he does. That does not convey to the reader because the reader cannot understand what you're talking about.

For example, let's say we get someone who is a great Cajun storyteller. He can tell the greatest story in the world. You cannot write that! You better not try to write it. Nobody's going to read it. Nobody can understand it. Even someone who knows what he's talking about can't understand a thing, so you don't write that that way.

I can take what he told me and say, OK, I'm going halfway with what he told me, and I'm going to get what I've learned from all these years of reading. Then I'm going to use proper syntax, I'm going to use proper spelling, I'm going to do all those other little things. I'm going to take from what he gave me, and I'm going to use things from my background. I'm going to use something from over here that I have, and then I'm going to combine these things and put it out there and pray that someone will understand.

CW: That it works.

GAINES: Yes, that it works.

CW: I think of that day we spent standing by the porch and listening to Reese talk. [Reese Spooner was an old man who lived in the quarters where Gaines grew up.]

GAINES: Damn right.

CW: He went through sixty or seventy years of the political history of Louisiana as he had seen it happen. You would have to do that in a dozen lines or a page and a half rather than two hours.

GAINES: Right. You can just take so much of what he's saying. That's what I was trying to do with Miss Jane Pittman, to get the essence of what she's saying. Then you use your background or you fill it in with the history. You fill it in with other things that you know.

CW: As we sat there and listened to old Reese talk, he obviously had a sense that the porch was a kind of a stage and we were his audience.

GAINES: Of course.

CW: You've said before that you write for your stories to be read aloud, that you more or less think your stories are being told in that kind of way. Do you have some sense of yourself as being the storyteller and the performer at the same time, the way Reese does when he's sitting on that porch talking to us?

GAINES: If you're saying entertaining through words is also performing, well, yeah. I have a sense somebody's going to read it, but I don't have a particular audience out there. I don't have any faces of anybody in mind when I'm writing it, but I feel that I'm writing to entertain, whether it's a comic scene or a tragic scene.

I must bring in some kind of reality to what my narrator is talking about. For example, if Reese is telling me a story and I want to repeat something he said, I have to do some research. If he's going to talk about the event of Huey Long's death—for example, I had to bring that in in *The Autobiography of Miss Jane Pittman*—I cannot just write what he says, because I'm not absolutely sure about what he says. So what I do is I go back and read something on this stuff. I've been listening to blacks talk about Long's death all my life, but I don't want to look like a damned fool by putting down what they said in a book. They might be telling me anything.

This is a very important thing when you write about Louisiana. You can mess up on Long's death—because everybody has messed up on Long's death. I can talk to everybody around here, and they're all going to tell me a different story about Long's death, why he died and how he died and all that sort of thing. So, after listening to everything these people had to say, I thought when I got ready to write that chapter, I'd better do some research. So I read T. Harry Williams' biography and I read *All the King's Men*—Robert Penn Warren's book—and Long's book, *Every Man a King*. I read newspaper clippings. I did all kinds of things. Then I went to the Louisiana Room at the LSU library and I went through page after page, manila folder after manila folder of things. Then I said, OK, I've got all this information, and now I must go back and give it to this little old lady back here, Miss

Jane. I've got to give her all this information, but I can't give her this information as I got it. I can't give her this information as a trained historian. I must in some way—and that's how we come back to the voice thing—give her all this information and let her tell this thing the way she would tell it, as an illiterate black woman a hundred years old talking about these things.

I must let *her* do it. It's like getting pork and putting it in the machine and grinding it up and grinding it up and grinding it up and letting it come out a different way from what it was when it was obtained. At the same time that I give her that information, I have to keep her in character. I cannot just give her hunks of history and throw them to her and have her describe, "It was Sunday, at seven o'clock and Huey Long was going from New Orleans to such and such a place, and the guy, [Carl A.] Weiss, comes from behind this pillar and shoots Long." I don't need all that because she never would have spoken that way. I would have been the one speaking that way. The historian would have been the one speaking that way. But I have to give her that information as if she were just holding a regular conversation with her friends sitting out on the porch. She doesn't know. She has heard this information from third or fourth or fifth persons. She's never read it in a book or a newspaper. She has just heard about it, and this is what she talks about.

So when you say what Reese is doing, I must have some idea of what Reese is talking about. He cannot just tell me anything. I must know what he's talking about. I, the writer, must know what he's talking about. See, my character Reese and Reese are two different people. Reese is a real man. My character is going to say what I want my character to say, but he's going to say it in the way that you think Reese would've said it. He's a character and he has to do what I want him to do, give you the information I want him to give you.

MG: Do you have a sense that that work is going to depend on how much you involve the reader, just as the oral storyteller has to involve the listener?

GAINES: Well, yes. I have to do something that can be understood. I have to do something that can be recognized. I have to write the proper kind of dialogue. I try to write dialogue in short sentences so you can grasp it. I try to make things as clear as possible. An actor or performer can make gestures or throw his voice out, and cry and weep and do all sorts of things like that. What I have to do is use those twenty-six letters that tell you these things.

CW: When the actor weeps or laughs, he's often trying to make his audience weep or laugh with him. Do you have a sense of trying to do that?

GAINES: I never think about making someone weep. I never think about making someone laugh. If I laugh at something I'm writing, I try to write it until I stop laughing, because I think then you'll get all the fun. You'll get the point of it. I don't try to make people weep or go out and act. If I write about a murder scene, I don't want anyone else to pick up a gun and go out and shoot somebody, but I try to make you feel it, and make you think, well, I would not want to be this kind of person, I don't want to be that, I want to be this.

CW: Do you want to involve the audience emotionally?

GAINES: I want the audience to see himself. I want the audience to see himself intellectually as well as emotionally.

CW: Are you also trying to disappear?

GAINES: I'm disappearing if I am writing from that first-person point of view. I'm totally disappearing because I must put everything into that character. That character has to be the entire person.

CW: What about in *Catherine Carmier* and *In My Father's House*? Were you trying to get the same kind of distance? Is the third-person voice as clear and separate, as distinct from you, as a first-person voice is?

GAINES: I don't think that it is, and that's why it's much more difficult for me to do. And I think it's much more difficult for American writers. I tell my students that what we've done with the first person is as great in literature as anything else we have done—any of our characters that we have created, any of the stories we have told, or anything else. I know that I'm not nearly as in control in the third-person omniscient as I am in the first person. If I get a character too close to me, I can't work with him. I'm having to deal with a character in this book I'm working on now. He's too damned close to me, and I'm having all kinds of problems. He's one of the reasons I'm not working as fast. He's too much like me. He's cynical at times. He hates things. He wants to say, "Goddamn it all. The hell with this stuff."

MG: Is he the narrator?

GAINES: He's the narrator. If I get a guy who just could go, I'm with him. I can say, "You take it. I don't want the ball anymore, so you carry the ball."

CW: Are you having trouble making the distinction between the character and the writer?

GAINES: It's not between the character and the writer. It's the voice. Not the person himself, but the voice. He speaks too much like me. You know you shouldn't let yourself think too much. It's good to just go on and do the work and stop all the damned thinking. When I come to the omniscient point of view and I create a character, a narrator who's much like myself, I do too much thinking. I don't have the freedom. That's one of the things I criticize *Invisible Man* about. There's too much thinking going on all the time. There's thinking in every goddamned sentence. You don't think. Let the thing flow. Let it go.

CW: That kind of thinking and that sort of trying to evaluate stops the story line.

GAINES: Yes, it impedes the movement of the story.

CW: One time you told us that you hoped your epitaph would be, "He was a good man who wrote well."

GAINES: That's right—that's all I wanted. When I write, I try to write well. I think that's the only way one should write. One should be proud enough to write well. If I were a painter, I would paint well, so someone could see the thing. I take more pride in what I do well than I care for what anyone else appreciates, takes from my work. Sometimes, really, I say, OK, I've done this. You like it? OK, good. You don't like it? I don't give a damn, because I do it well. That's all I want to do, just do my work well. I'd want my friends to read it. I'd read a chapter, say, to Carl, and say, "OK, man, what do you think of this?" Carl might say, "Well, it's the shits." Well, so what? I think it's good. Really, I never think of an audience. I just think of getting something down that is good and then having it published. I want someone to buy it, of course, because that's how I support myself. Friendship or whatever, I do as well as I possibly can, and that's it. And if I can get along with you by doing it well, good. If I can't get along with you by doing it well, I don't care anymore.

MG: You wouldn't change your writing to make people buy it.

GAINES: No way! No way will I change, no! People have asked me quite often, "Who do you write for?" I say I don't write for any particular group. But if there's a gun put to my head and someone says, "OK, name somebody you write for," I'd say, "I write for the black youth of the South." And if there are two groups, I'd say, "I write for the black and white youth of the South." Those are the people I would write for.

Number one, I would want the black youth to say, "Hey, I am somebody." And I'd want the white youth to say, "Hey, that is part of me out there, and I can only understand myself truly if I can understand my neighbor." That's the only way one can understand himself, if he can understand other things around him. We live—you know, Donne's "No man is an island" and "Don't ask for whom the bell tolls"—Every little piece of things around us makes us a little bit whole. We can go through the world being half people, and most of us do that most of our lives. But in order to understand more about ourselves and the world, we must understand what's around. So that's what I'd want: the white kids to understand what the black kid is, and the black kid to understand who he is, if I had to write for any group. *Jane Pittman* has been translated into Chinese. I did not write for the Chinese. *Miss Jane Pittman* has been translated into Japanese, Russian, German, and two or three other languages. *A Gathering of Old Men* just came out in German, and it will come out in Russian next year. I'm not writing for them, but I try to write as well as I possibly can and just hope the readers come from wherever they come from.

MG: What you say reminds me of Faulkner's statement that what he's really concerned about are the concerns of the human heart. You're just interested in writing well, and you hope that what you write will appeal to anyone who is concerned about humanity.

GAINES: True! And if you write well and true enough, you're going to find that a little old lady in China, a little lady in Russia or in Japan, will see that and say, "Oh, you know, yeah." Not all of the little things that happened to Miss Jane, but one of the little things or two of the little things that happened, that person can see herself in it. So you try to write as truly and as deeply and understandably about the human condition as you possibly can. That's all you can do. There's nothing else to do.

CW: You've been doing this for a good while now.

GAINES: I've been at it for about thirty years.

CW: Your books are striking in both their dissimilarities and their similarities to one another. They take on very different subjects, but you have a lot of recurring things in your books, some basic metaphors and characters and images. Do these come out of both your own experience and your literary background as well? Do you have a sense of them, also, as maybe being a part of the culture that you're sharing with your reader when you put these things down?

GAINES: It's knowing the place, knowing the people, and then letting your imagination take over to a certain point. In all of the books I've written, I've centered my stories around the Pointe Coupée Parish, West Baton Rouge area, and that would be my locale. The themes would be in search of manhood, or standing as a man at a certain point in time, and the old people, how they're connected to the land, and how the younger people are reacting to that, whether or not they want to accept this connection and carry a burden, or move on and take a chance.

CW: You've talked before about influences or models that you emulated, in the manner that Hemingway says he did with Twain, and Norris did with Zola.

GAINES: You do emulate when you start out. I started out in the libraries, and I was just reading everything in my late teens in libraries. But I was fortunate, when I came out of the army, that I had some very good teachers who were just coming into San Francisco at that time. They were eager to help, and they were just coming out from the Korean War. At that same time we had the Beat scene going on in San Francisco, so we were reading a lot of books. And once my teachers saw what I wanted to write about—that was about rural Louisiana, and this was in the mid-fifties—they encouraged me and recommended writers and stories to read.

I also discovered how music can help, and as Hemingway suggested, paintings can help, just by going to a museum or art gallery. Just look at paintings and see how you can describe a beautiful room with only two or three things in that room, without having to go through everything in the room. Right now I'm thinking of Van Gogh's painting called *Vincent's Room*—it's the room where he used to live and sleep—and how he could do it so well with only two or three things or pieces of things in that room.

I've also learned from the discipline of great athletes, by just watching them. I ran a lot of track myself. I was the worst football player ever put a helmet on his head, but I was pretty good at track in college. But I know about the discipline of athletes, and I know that same discipline must pertain to the writer, to the artist. He must be disciplined. He must do things over and over and over and over and over. And these kinds of things are also a great influence. The grace-under-pressure thing I think I learned from Hemingway.

I learned much about dialogue from Faulkner, especially when we're dealing with our southern dialects. I learned rhythms and things from Gertrude Stein, learned to put a complete story in a day from Joyce's *Ulysses*, or Tolstoy's "The Death of Ivan Ilyich."

CW: You have said that you learned form from the Russians.

GAINES: I started out with form from Ivan Turgenev. I was very much impressed, not only with form but with their use of peasantry, how they used their serfs. And I think their serfs are used much more humanely in their fiction than, say, the slaves were used, or the blacks were used, by many of the southern writers. I remember Tolstoy says, you just watch a serf, just watch him. He'll never tell you the truth. He's going all the way around this thing. He says, now if you watch closely, you'll figure out the truth, but, boy, he's going to lead you all through the swamps, all through the woods, and then you get it. Then you get the truth out of him. And I learned that from just listening to these guys tell a story.

CW: Many writers claim that they're trying to create order out of all the chaos and disorder in the world. Do you have a sense of doing that?

GAINES: I try. I think art is order. I think art must be order, no matter what you do with it. I don't care what Picasso did with twisted faces and bodies—all of that sort of thing—I think there has to be a form of order there, or it's not art. The novel to me is art. The short story is art. And there must be order. I don't care what the chaos is. You must put it in some kind of decent form. When you leave this thing, you say you've gone through war, you've gone through hell, but this is not hell. This is a piece of art. This is work. This is a picture of hell. After reading this, you felt something very—not good about hell—something good about this piece of work. This is all it takes.

CW: Another term I've heard you use in a slightly different way is *work*. What do you mean when you talk to students about what work really means to a writer?

GAINES: Well, I think if we're dealing with time, physical work is getting up and working at the desk. But I would think that a writer never stops working as long as he is conscious. As long as he is awake, he is thinking about his work. And then he sits down four or five hours, six hours, whatever he does a day, and does his work there. Work means having your antennae out, too—that you're tuned in. And, as Hemingway once said—I have a lot of Hemingway quotes—a writer must have a built-in shit detector. He must know when someone is bullshitting him. He really must. He must know what's going on. He must know fact from fiction. He must know when someone's pulling his leg. He must know, when someone is touching him on the back, whether it's a good touch. Whether it's a good handshake. He has to have this kind of awareness of things. So the writer is always working. But maybe in "work," I mean discipline and sitting down at that desk.

MG: A writer is always observing people.

GAINES: He is. Well, it's not observing people. He's being. People used to ask me, "Say, why do you go back to Louisiana from California?" And I'd say, I'd go back to Louisiana just to be. I never did come back here with a microscope and say, OK, put your hand under here, I want to see skin color and all that sort of thing. I never did just stare at people and say, "There's a man over there, and he's five feet eight, nine inches tall." But when I'd come back, I'd come back just to be back and then, if I went to a cafe to eat, something would come into me. I don't have to look at the place and say, well, OK, this is a little thing I'm going to put down. But if I'm there, something will happen, the color of the oilcloth on the table—you know those checkered oilcloths—whether blue and white or red and white or red and black, something would happen, and unconsciously I'd become aware of it. I'd become aware of the taste of the food. All this sort of thing, because your antennae are out. You're not staring at things, but you're— [Pause]

MG: You're sort of absorbing it.

GAINES: You're absorbing it, yes.

CW: Do you ever get so involved with the fictional world that you're creating that you sometimes have difficulty telling the difference between that one and the one you're walking around in?

GAINES: No, I don't. But when I was writing *Catherine Carmier*—and, I think, *Of Love and Dust*—I used to pray to God to turn it off sometime, because I would be so involved that I could not rest. And I didn't care for anything else. And I would just say: "Listen, I'd rather be just a poor writer. If I have to go through this hell to be a good writer, please turn it off. I just can't take any more of this stuff. I'd rather be just poor and ordinary, just one of the other guys, you know, but just turn it off." But I don't think I've ever reached the point where I was unaware of my surroundings. I've never been in the place that I was writing about.

CW: I ask that because the first time you took me to the quarters, you talked about people and pointed out houses where they lived. Without making any distinction between them, you talked about the houses of real people and of characters in your novels.

GAINES: Yes. Oh, sure.

CW: Then you have that sense of them having that kind of a reality?

GAINES: Oh, yes. Oh, yes. For example, I took someone down there a couple of weeks ago, and I just said, "Well, there's Miss Jane Pittman's, right by there." My grandmother lived there, you know, but I said Miss Jane Pittman lived there. And I said, "Now, behind those trees over there, that house does not exist anymore, but that's where Catherine lived." [Gaines laughs.] You have nothing but those oak trees there now. And that also would be the place where Bonbon [the overseer in *Of Love and Dust*] would have stayed, you know, so I say he lived there. And this is where Marcus would be raking those leaves, under this tree over here.

MG: You said earlier that music helped you develop as a writer. How has music helped you?

GAINES: During the time I was writing *The Autobiography of Miss Jane Pittman*, I was playing Moussorgsky's *Pictures at an Exhibition*. It's about someone going to a museum or art gallery and looking at pictures against the wall. There are different kinds of pictures—dramatic pictures, comic pictures, different colors—all depicted in sound. There is a common motif going through the whole thing. At one time when I was writing *The Autobiography of Miss Jane Pittman*, I was thinking about sketches of a plantation because I had been listening to that so much. I was thinking sketches, sketches, sketches, and then I ceased thinking of sketches, for *The Autobiography*.

Another thing about music: I think some of the best descriptions, especially dealing with blacks, some of the best descriptions of the big flood of '27, which most southern writers have written about, have been described better in music, especially by great blues singers like Bessie Smith, Josh White, Leadbelly, and many other great blues singers. They described the black situation much better than the whites did. The whites did the newspaper things at that time, but when it came down to the more intimate things, I think the black blues singers gave us better descriptions even than the black writers did at that particular time. Another thing, especially in jazz music, is a repetition of things, repeating and repeating to get the point over, which I try to do in dialogue. Another thing I learned from music is something that Hemingway also does, and that is understatement. Certain musicians, like Lester Young—one of the greatest jazz saxophonists—could play around a note. For example, if he were playing "Stardust," he didn't have to go through the old beat-after-beat of "Stardust." He could give you a feeling of "Stardust" by playing around the note. Instead of playing on the note, he plays around the note, or under the note, or above the note, but he still gives you those feelings.

I tried to explain that in one interview when we did "The Sky Is

Gray" for the film. In "The Sky Is Gray," the mother and her child must go to town to get the tooth pulled. They must sit in an all-black waiting room. They can't have any food or drink or anything "up-town." They must go "back-of-town" in order to eat or drink. Now, if I had wanted to hit the nail on the head, I could have put them in a white restaurant and had them thrown out, but by the fact that they have to go back-of-town, you know that they would not have been accepted uptown. So I'm not saying, "Go in here and get thrown out," but instead I'm saying, "Go back-of-town to eat." This is what they would have had to do. The only whites they come in contact with are people who are kind to them—the old lady who gives them food at the very end, and the place where she can go in and pretend to buy an axe handle, so the kid can warm himself. It's not hitting the nail on the head, but playing around it. I think this is much more effective. And I learned a lot of that from reading Hemingway, and I learned a lot of that from listening to certain jazz musicians.

MG: We know that you have a large collection of jazz albums, and you have commented before that you usually play music when you're writing. Do you still do that?

GAINES: Oh, yes. Whether I'm playing jazz or classical music, or just listening to the radio, I usually have music in the background, but soft, so it does not disturb me. I have to keep music. It relaxes me, and at the same time it gives me a sense of rhythm, of beat.

MG: Do you think maybe it gives you the atmosphere, or the kind of feeling, you want?

GAINES: I don't know that it sets a mood or anything like that. I think I have to sort of build myself to the mood myself before I begin to write. And yet, at times, it can. It's possible that when I was writing *The Autobiography of Miss Jane Pittman*, because I played *Pictures at an Exhibition* just about every day while I was writing it—two years, I guess—maybe I needed that to get started. But sometimes I play music just for the background, but soft in the background. I don't play Beethoven's Fifth because that's too disturbing. I play some sort of soft music, violin or cello or whatever, as sort of the background. It's just like you need water or coffee around the place, you know. You have some music in the background to keep you going that day, I guess.

CW: How was music present in your world as you were growing up?

GAINES: Well, of course, I came from a plantation. There was a church not very far from our house. I could hear the people singing all the time. I had to go to Sunday school and church as a child, and, of course, the people sang. I could never carry a tune myself, but the old ones did. And my mother sang, and my aunt. I didn't hear classical music or anything like that. I don't think the radio worked half the time, but there was always music, somebody doing something.

MG: And was it typical of people to be singing—for your mother to be singing?

GAINES: Yes, while they were working. People sang when they were working.

CW: So far you've described the indirect importance music has had in your writing. Do you ever see it creeping in more directly, through musical language or musical references?

GAINES: Oh, no. I don't think I ever use music, really, like that. In *Of Love and Dust*, Jim has a guitar. I think in "The Sky Is Gray," the young kid, James, thinks back on the old man who plays a guitar around the house. When I was a small child, we did have a man like that who played the guitar around the place. But I don't know anything about music. I can't read music at all. I remember when I had to do the reading of the *Portrait of Lincoln* with the USL orchestra, I explained to the conductor, "I don't know one note of music, so whenever you want me to start reading, you just nod your head." We had a record of Carl Sandburg reading it, so I could figure out the rhythm and speed, the way the thing should be read. But I couldn't follow the notes and all on paper. I don't know a thing about music.

2
Finding the Voice

MG: Humor is very much a part of your writing, but do you feel that your vision is an essentially comic, optimistic one?

GAINES: I don't really know that I'm very optimistic. I think, in much black folklore and blues, that even when things are at their worst, there's often something humorous that comes through. Even with tough, hard men whose lives are really rough, something funny at times can happen. I don't know that I'm pessimistic about life, but I don't know that I'm terribly optimistic either. I see lots of things as being humorous, even if it's in a ridiculous way. When people take advantage of people, or when people hurt other people, it's often just ridiculous, and the humor comes through. My characters are not usually 100 percent bitter, not hardened to the point that they cannot feel and give and change. Humor and joking are part of change. I don't know that it is a sign of optimism in my work. I can't go that far.

CW: There is no real optimism about the system or the social structure in your work. Bad things happen to people, often because of the system, as in *Of Love and Dust*. Even in *A Gathering of Old Men*, the good that occurs happens through the individuals who are willing to go against the system. There does seem to be a premise that men and women are capable of the courage to do what they ought to do, in spite of the system. Do you sometimes see that capability in terms of the Hemingway theme of grace under pressure, which you have often remarked about?

GAINES: I've always said to students, especially black students, that somehow I feel that Hemingway was writing more about blacks than he was, really, about whites when he was using the grace-under-pressure theme. I see that Hemingway usually put his people in a moment where they must have grace under pressure, and I've often looked at black life not only as a moment, but more as something constant, everyday. This is what my characters must come through.

CW: What about Hemingway's other themes? Such as futility and the general pointlessness of life sometimes.

GAINES: It's his structure of paragraphs, his structure of sentences, the dialogue, of course. Hemingway can repeat the lighting of a cigarette, the length or shortness of the cigarette, or the ash hanging, to show how time moves. He repeats little things throughout a scene to make you know the movement of time. These are the kinds of things I read carefully in his work. I think Hemingway's importance to me is a combination of the language and that particular theme of grace under pressure. Of course, there are also his drinking well and eating well. I like to do that, too.

CW: You've mentioned also the influence of Twain, both his humor and his form.

GAINES: Twain's humor and his folktales, the humorous story within a story—these are the kinds of things that I think have had some influence on me. With Faulkner, it's also the humor of the story within the story, the breaking up of the dramatic thing with humor. Not that it's intentionally put there, but it happens. That goes back to what we were saying about humor a moment ago, and that is that no matter how hard life is, something funny is going to happen.

MG: You do that in "Three Men" with Munford's tall tale about the preacher. You see that humor is very much a part of the folk tradition.

GAINES: Yes. You see, I'm not a naturalistic writer. I'm not a person who will stick to detail after detail as a scientist would, as the naturalist writers would—as, say, Wright's *Native Son* or Dreiser's *Sister Carrie* or *An American Tragedy*. I'm not that kind of a writer, that I stick to that direct dramatic theme. The humor has to come in somewhere.

MG: You often contrast the stereotype of the frightened black man with the rebellious young man to show what things were really like, how they overcame, how they coped.

GAINES: There's constant contrast in just about everything. For example, in *Of Love and Dust*, there's Bishop and there's Marcus. Bishop is the guy who sits back, and Marcus says: "Not me. I never did know these things were happening, until someone started saying these things happened. And then I began to see them." In "The Sky Is

Gray," you have the student and the minister, absolute opposites. You'll find those who'll go along with the traditional stuff. They'll go along with it because this is what the world is supposed to be. And the other guy says: "I can't do that. In order to change I must rebel completely against what you're standing for over there." Usually the coward is a minor figure, and quite often he is a comic figure. The more bold, the braver person is usually the protagonist, the person who must make the changes, the person who must step over that line. While the other fellow stays back, this person steps over the line, and he's the guy who makes the changes.

MG: Others have observed that, in *A Gathering of Old Men*, it is the white man who becomes the comic figure—the little deputy sheriff [Griffin], and then Mapes himself becomes a comic figure that the black people laugh at because they're controlling him. He's not controlling them.

GAINES: I think, in Griffin's case, he is a comic character. I wanted to make him an ignorant little fellow. I think Mapes's humor comes through much more. Not that Mapes is beaten, but I think Mapes's humor comes through change. Mapes becomes a much more human being, and once he becomes more of a human being, he becomes more humorous. I think that deep inside of him he's got these qualities, but it takes a time to bring those qualities out of him. I'm sure when Mapes would get around with his own kind, before that particular day, Mapes would be one of the most humorous guys around that place. He'd probably tell jokes—drinking and telling jokes and all kinds of stuff like that. That's the kind of guy he would be, but when he came into the black quarters, he's a different person altogether. Then when he runs into these old men—these men are in their seventies, and they've seen their lives already and would not mind dying today—then it's his humanity that comes out. When he sees these guys are men after all, then his humanity comes out.

CW: I don't get the sense that he becomes the comic figure to the black characters in the story as much as he does to those of us who are watching both him and the black characters. It's the audience to whom Mapes becomes a comic figure. The blacks really aren't laughing at him.

GAINES: No, they're not. The only time they would be laughing at Mapes is when he's sitting down there. They're not really laughing at him then, because the only person who really sees him is Snookum. I never really thought of Mapes as being a comic character as much as I thought of him as being a more human person, when he realizes what's going on. I think the other people can laugh at Mapes because they realize how absurd he is, how ridiculous he is, just wanting to get information by beating up on people and all that sort of thing. And I don't think they would have thought he was absurd except for that one day, see, because probably in the days before that, they were afraid of him. They feared a person like Mapes. And that afternoon they just felt like, well, OK, we finally realized just how absurd this whole idea is.

Although I never get into Mathu's brain, I think Mathu would have been the guy who really could understand Mapes as well as anyone else could. He would have known his weakness. They hunted a lot together. He would have known that Mapes could not shoot straight all the time, or he could not do one of these things all the time, and Mathu could do it just as well. And Mapes probably told Mathu things, just like Sidney Bonbon told Jim things in *Of Love and Dust*. He'd tell him some things, but maybe he'd draw back, you know. Jim could see the weakness in Bonbon, just as Mathu, if I had gone into his mind, could have seen the weakness in Mapes and realized what Mapes was about.

CW: Even though you didn't give Mathu a voice, in order to give those other people their voices you really had to know what was going on inside Mathu.

GAINES: Oh, yes. I knew Mathu. Just as I knew Mapes all the time. I didn't give Mapes a voice either, but I knew Mapes all the time. Everything about him. I knew what he was.

MG: Students often don't realize that Mathu doesn't have a voice, because they hear it so plainly.

CW: The others come to realize what Mathu already knows.

GAINES: Just like in the story "Just Like a Tree," the old lady who's leaving, Aunt Fe, doesn't have a voice, but everything comes from her.

MG: *A Gathering of Old Men* is told with fifteen different voices—

GAINES: I'm glad somebody counted them, because I didn't know.

CW: Yes, but in the book, the two people who are really central to everything that's going on are Candy and Mathu, and you don't give either of them their own voices. Why not?

GAINES: Because they have to lie to tell anything that goes on. Maybe Candy doesn't, but Mathu would have to lie.

MG: He knows too much.

GAINES: Mathu knows what happened. And if we start using Mathu's voice and he doesn't tell you what happened, then we're going to say, well, wait a while.

CW: You've tricked the reader.

GAINES: We're tricking you, and I'd rather not trick you. I'd rather lay off completely away from it before I'd trick you.

CW: One of the effects of coming at Mathu and Candy by indirection rather than through their own voices is to heighten our sense of their involvement.

GAINES: When I first read it here, in '78, everything was told from the point of view of the white reporter, Lou Dimes. I think I must have written it two or three times from Lou Dimes's point of view. In one of the first writings from the multiple point of view, I had Mapes telling part of it. Remember in the story, when Mapes comes there, he keeps telling them, "I want to go fishing." Well, Mapes was leaving to go fishing when Griffin catches up with him. I had Griffin beating on the car in front of the courthouse: "Hey, Mapes, Mapes, there's been a murder." And Mapes says, "Hell with it. Let Russell take over." And Mapes is going fishing—Griffin is holding onto the car, and Mapes is dragging him. That draft is in Dupre Library [at the University of Southwestern Louisiana]. I also had Lou starting out from Baton Rouge. Then my editor says, OK, we don't need all these people leaving and coming here. We just want a couple of the old men—I had *all* the old men leaving from home. So then it was cut down and cut down and cut down. That's where your editor comes in. He'll say, OK, let's cut out some of these things and just have them showing up.

MG: I think that's fascinating to students, that this didn't come out all at once, that it was done in many different versions until, finally, you came up with the way you really wanted it.

GAINES: That's another thing about the writing, when you ask me how do you write and how do you do these things. I've tried in the novels as well as in the short stories to take different points of view. Not only have I had certain themes, but I've approached them from different points of view, the multiple, the first-person, as well as the omniscient.

CW: You have two novels in which you set up a basically third-person, omniscient point of view. You have three novels in which you use primarily a first-person point of view. At the same time, you don't have any one novel that uses the same narrative technique or the same narrative framework that any of the other novels uses. All five of them use a different narrative technique.

GAINES: What's the difference between the technique of *Catherine Carmier* and *In My Father's House*?

CW: In *Catherine Carmier* you start doing some of the things that you do later, as in *Of Love and Dust*. You have other people, like the old people sitting on the porch, like the old woman who knows what—

GAINES: Yeah. Madame Bayonne.

CW: —and Aunt Charlotte, who is sitting on the porch and observing things. Even though it's all done in the third person, you have this other person who is kind of seeing things and telling things from a particular perspective. They're not there in *In My Father's House*. We really don't have that other way of looking at the story through somebody else's eyes. You do that kind of thing in all the others, too, but you do it differently in each one.

GAINES: Ah, yes. Well, see, I don't know these things. [Laughter]

CW: The first-person point of view is very important to you, but you have different kinds of first-person points of view. How do you search for and find the voice you have to have to tell the particular story?

GAINES: In *Of Love and Dust*, which is the first of the first-person point of view novels, I knew Marcus could not tell the story.

He was too much involved in it. I had to find someone believable. He has to be acceptable. Even if he has to use tricks, he has to be able to communicate. Huckleberry Finn used all kinds of little tricks to communicate with all kinds of people and find out little things he needs to find out about. Nick Carraway, in *The Great Gatsby*, has to be someone who can communicate with Gatsby and the superrich Daisy and her husband and their crowd. You search for a character who's believable, who is somewhat likable—he can be a rascal, but he's believable—and who can communicate with different levels. And if he can't, he must find someone else to help him communicate to the audience. He must find that person. He must run into someone, he must create someone. I mean that writer has to create someone. Character A cannot possibly reach Character C, so you must create a Character B to communicate from Character C to Character A. Then Character A can take it back to the reader. You must do that. Now, I don't do things like, "This is Character A, this is Character B, this is Character C." Once I get involved in it, I'm just like a Shakespearean messenger. I get messages out there. Somebody's going to bring a letter on the stage right now to get this stage clear for the next act. Somebody must come and do this for me.

CW: Obviously, in *Of Love and Dust*, you set yourself up with what might appear to some an impossible problem. How in the world can Jim know what's going on in that bedroom? Or how can he know how Marcus gets Louise to come down to the fence to talk to him? He doesn't have any way of knowing.

GAINES: Of course! These are the kinds of things that you must invent something believable for. Number one, you believe in Jim. You believe in Jim as a decent guy who is coming to you and telling you what is going on. Jim gets along with everybody else. He gets along with Marcus very, very well. He's got to get along with Marcus because that's the only way he's going to tell Marcus' story. To create Jim, he has to be a believable person. He has to be a kind of guy that you can say, well, he can be weak or something like that—I don't like him all the time—but I believe this guy. I believe what this guy is telling me. So Aunt Margaret has to tell him about things, and Aunt Margaret tells things from sound. Margaret doesn't see a thing in that bedroom.

That's one of the techniques. Another technique that I've learned is from radio, where you can only hear things and they tell you what's going on. You know, all the old fifties radio stories—"This is happening on the fiftieth floor of the Fairmont Hotel, and it's foggy out there." You don't do things like that, but I mean the guy had to build up the atmosphere, and build up everything, for you to see what was going on in their stories. And when it came to writing it down, I learned a lot from listening to radio.

But you create a believable character. You must create that believable character to communicate to your reader. And once you do that, you can use tricks. Every writer uses some sort of tricks or another, every damned writer. Shakespeare used them. Faulkner uses them. Anybody who uses the first-person point of view has to use tricks, because the limitation of the first-person point of view is that that person can't be there all the time. And you say, OK, he can't be there at all times, so how am I going to get this message to my reader? Now I must create an incident that's believable. It can't be too ridiculous. It can be just little bits brought into my story. But I must get that information and bring it to my reader.

CW: Can you elaborate a little bit on tricks?

GAINES: Well, the trick is that Aunt Margaret must hear it for Jim to tell it. Without Aunt Margaret being there, Jim can't tell the story. Without Sun Brown coming down the quarters at that particular time, he can't see Marcus and Louise at the fence. I have to create Sun Brown. These are the little tricks. But the tricks must be subtle, too. We can't just write "big thick trick," you know.

CW: The scene that's only being heard also gives the opportunity for humor, because she has to interpret it to Jim. It's funny just thinking about all that's going on in the bedroom, and her sitting out there and having to listen to it. And she has to explain it to Jim and tell the child [the girl Tite] something the child will accept, without telling her what's really going on.

GAINES: Of course, and she can't possibly tell Jim all that's going on. Jim has to interpolate what she's saying. She's saying, "You know what I heard?" and Jim's saying, "Oh, she heard noises and all like that." She's not telling him everything. She's not giving him all the little explicit details. Jim's watching her gestures, he's watching her face. But we take all that out. Jim is seeing beyond what she's saying. Jim is reading between the lines. This is an old woman. This old woman is not going to explain these explicit sex sounds and all that kind of stuff. Jim has to read between all the things that she says, and then he gives it to you, yes.

CW: When you take these two voices and combine them, it becomes almost like an omniscient voice, almost like a third-person kind of thing. We've been talking about where your narrator is in order to tell the story, but that leads to speculation about where you are as a writer: what your sense of this narrating character is, and how this is happening.

GAINES: I don't think I'm there at all. One of the things Jim says as he's driving his tractor is, God doesn't care anymore. He's up there playing cards. He's playing solitaire by himself and saying, "Now, you guys do anything you want down there. I've done all I can do. You people are going to do it anyhow, so just do what you want to do and include me out!"

CW: Then you do not see yourself as Thackeray saw himself, as a puppeteer constantly pulling the strings.

GAINES: No, no. No, no. I try not to do that. I try to avoid it. One of the things that I've always criticized about Ellison's *Invisible Man* is that Ellison is always the puppeteer. He's always there. You never lose him. And that is not the way, especially in this picaresque novel. That thing is supposed to take over, and you're not supposed to sense that writer ever again. That thing's supposed to just take over and go! You stay away from those people and let those people do. Unless they just become ridiculous, and then you say, "OK, now, you don't do that."

CW: When we read *The Autobiography of Miss Jane Pittman*, we read it in the past tense. Jane tells it in the past tense, and we see her as a character in the past. But as you were talking about it, you said your problem was how to take information, about Huey Long for example, the way you learned it, to this little old lady who is—and you used the term *who is* as though she's sitting right here, right now. Do you have a sense of her being in the present, just as Reese was sitting on the porch when he was talking to us?

GAINES: Oh, yes. She's giving information to that newspaper guy. Well, you know, in my novel he's a black schoolteacher from Baton Rouge and not a white journalist from New York. But she's talking to him, just as we're talking now, and she's telling him what went on. She's speaking to a tape recorder, just as we're speaking to a tape recorder now, and she's telling him what goes on. What he would have to do, though, is he would have to crank up her mind and make her get back there. And once he got her mind working, she would get back there, she would live that past. So the present is forgotten completely. You forget the present, but he had to do that every time he came back to visit her.

CW: Did you have to do that every time you started writing?

GAINES: No, I think I just picked up from the past. I don't think I had to do it. Once I started with the teacher, he was ignored; I forgot about him altogether. I just knew that an old person would not tell a story that way, so I had to get him to say: "Listen, I had to do a lot of correction. I had to check some things here. I'm giving you the essence of what she talked about. But I can't tell you everything, because I'd have volumes all over this place. I can only give you the essence of what she said." However, when I started writing, I didn't want him anywhere present. I wanted her to talk about the past and ignore him, just cut him completely out of it. For example, like you would come here and you would talk to me, and I would tell you something that would happen back there, but I would cut you out of there altogether. I'd just go along with the story, move the story along chronologically from the point of view of whoever is telling the story. I think it's the same sort of thing Conrad does in *Heart of Darkness*. And Faulkner would do it so well, but all of a sudden Faulkner would come back into the present, with the guys squatting there and somebody telling his story, and then he'd go back to what he was talking about. You know, he'd just smell whatever the flowers were at that time around the house. I forget the kind of flowers he had around the house. But what I did was I just cut out that scene where the flowers come in and just stick to that other thing back there.

MG: One of the things that amazes me about *The Autobiography of Miss Jane Pittman* is that it so realistically portrays what folklorists find in talking to older people. Once you get them started, you bring it to mind—they're not talking to the machine and they're not talking to you.

GAINES: Remember, now, I put other old people with her. I put her there, and I put several others around her on the porch, just as we are here. You get her talking; she is the central part of it. But the others would come in on the thing. For example, in the beginning of the film when you see [Gaines here slumps over into the posture of a much older person, and his voice rises in pitch and trembles as he speaks], "Aunt Lena, when I don't know, you recall things." Well, that's good, too. I mean, they need something like that for a film, you know. But he would have to do this every day on which he visited her. He would have to do it every day. All I do is just leave it all out, just cut it out, say, "Well, I won't have that in there."

I did it at one time. I had a different approach. I had two or three students visiting this old woman, not one teacher but two or three students visiting this old woman. I think there were four of them altogether. I think there were two whites and two blacks, and they had all kinds of discussions about what this old lady was talking about and all this sort of thing. The story was about them coming from Baton Rouge and coming to this plantation each time they visited it. And I said, "Aw, that stuff is no good."

MG: That was a different story.

GAINES: It was a different story altogether, because the reader started focusing on the problems between these students. So I just cut all that out. I just put that aside and just followed her story. You find that in movies, flashbacks. They do it all the time.

MG: Earlier, you mentioned *Huckleberry Finn*. The novel has been attacked as a racist book. What do you think of the claim that it is a racist book?

GAINES: I don't pay too much attention to these things when these things happen around me. I know when I read it, I never thought of it as a racist novel. I haven't read it recently, and I suppose if I were to read it again, I would look for those kinds of signs in the book. When I read the book twenty years ago, or fifteen years ago, I didn't see it as racist. I never did see it that way. That's about the only thing

I can say about it. I don't think Twain was being more critical of blacks in that book than he was of a certain white mentality. He was dealing with how evil some men can be toward other men. I think that Twain was terribly critical of society. That's what the whole thing was all about. It wasn't as much antiblack as it was anti the established society at that time. I avoid these kinds of things. As I said, when I read the book, I did not see those signs. If I read the book all over again, looked for certain things, and talked with people with whom I can discuss a work like that, then I could ask a person, "What do you think of this passage or that passage?" And maybe I could say, whoever said this was a racist book has a point. But sitting here now, I can't recall any passage that points toward racism in the novel.

CW: You've talked a great deal about Hemingway, Twain, Faulkner, and the Russian writers, who have had a very great influence on you. You also said that when you became a writer, one of the things that influenced you was that you couldn't find stories by and about black people. Which black writers do you think had some influence on you?

GAINES: No black writer had influence on me. I went to California when I was fifteen years old. Of course, I had not read any books here in Louisiana. If there were books there in the libraries, I would not have been allowed to go there, but I doubt that there were books by blacks at that time in the libraries around New Roads. When I went to California, I went to a small town. I went to Vallejo instead of San Francisco, but even there, there were not too many books by black writers. All of my reading—even if I wanted to read about peasant life—turned out to be by white writers.

When I went to college, I studied white writers. We're talking about the early fifties. Richard Wright was probably the most well-known black writer at that time, but his novel *Native Son* was not taught. Passages would be brought up in the class, why Bigger does what he does type of stuff, why he is angry, and all this sort of thing. *Invisible Man* had just come out, but it was not in the curriculum yet. You did not read *Invisible Man* as a part of American literature at that time. At a place like San Francisco State at that time, you were still reading Hemingway, reading Faulkner. You were not reading the black writers then as you would be ten years later. When I was developing as a writer, the books were not there. They were not being taught in the classroom, and only a few of them were there. As I said, *Native Son* and *Black Boy* were there, *Uncle Tom's Children*, and *Invisible Man* had just come out. Baldwin's essays were just being read, but they were not being taught. They were just there.

At that particular time, I was so far behind the average kid I had to go to school with, because I had not read anything. I was still catching up, so I did not have time to go out and read anything other than what I was assigned to read. They'd say read "Dry September" this week for this class; read "Dry September" and read Twain's *Huckleberry Finn*. When the black novels were not taught, I didn't have the chance to go out and get them. If I could have found them, I didn't have the chance to go out and read them. So black writers had no influence on me at all. One book—and I've said this many times before—one book by a black writer that would have had as much influence on me as any other book would be *Cane*, by Jean Toomer. What he does in those short chapters are things that I wish I could do today, those little short chapters, those little songs, the poetry between the chapters. That is still my favorite novel of any black writer.

MG: You've said many times that Louisiana is your area. Do you think maybe Toomer would have influenced you because he was writing about the same kinds of things and about the southern area?

GAINES: I think it may have been subject matter as well as structure. I like that kind of structure, putting the short chapters together to make a novel. Of course, I try to do that in the *Bloodline* stories, getting all these things together to make a novel, like Faulkner did in *Go Down, Moses*. It would be theme and structure in *Cane*, but especially structure. One of the good things that happened when I was studying writing at San Francisco State, as well as at Stanford, was they taught me technique, not telling me what to write, but how to write it and how to write it better. I was not pushed with a lot of political ideas. I was not pushed with demands to write about race or anything else. They said write what you want to write about, bring it in, and we'll discuss. And they discussed it more from a technical point of view. I try to teach now from a technical point of view. My students can write about anything they want. I don't care what they write about, born-again Christian, Klansman, or anything you want to write about, as long as you write well. If you don't write well, then I have to criticize it. And fortunately, that was what I needed at the time.

I always knew what I wanted to do. I had to find a way in which to do it. For example, before I wrote "The Sky Is Gray," I had to read Eudora Welty. I was assigned once to read "A Worn Path," and I thought, "This is a great story." I read "A Worn Path" at least ten years before I wrote "The Sky Is Gray." When I went to write "The Sky Is Gray," I knew a model, just as I did in "A Long Day in November," with the first part of Faulkner's *The Sound and the Fury*. These are the kinds of things I learned, and these are the kinds of things they were helping me with, [Wallace] Stegner at Stanford and Stanley Anderson and Mark Harris at San Francisco State. They were telling me to read these things. I don't know that any black writer could have helped me any more, technically.

MG: Did you ever read Zora Neale Hurston?

GAINES: I did not read her until later, as I read Wright later. I read Ellison later. I read Langston Hughes later. I didn't read *Cane* until after I got out of college. I didn't read *Cane* until about '59 or '60. By then I had developed what I suppose is my way of writing.

MG: One of the reasons Hurston came to mind is that, in all the times you've talked about influences, there doesn't seem to be any mention of any woman writer, other than what you have said about Eudora Welty.

GAINES: Well, I mentioned just that one story by Eudora Welty.

CW: It seems like an almost incredible working of chance to consider the differences between your work and the works of many other black writers that resulted from the fact that when you left the South, you went west and the others went north. You went to San Francisco, and they went to Chicago and Detroit and New York, so that you evidence a totally different sense of what it was—leaving the South and going to something very different from what the others went to.

GAINES: Well, I went to a small town, too: Vallejo. Say if I had gone to Los Angeles and gone to Watts, it would have been a different thing altogether. A big city where there was a total black ghetto could have been a different thing altogether. But I went to a small town in northern California, and the people who were in this town—the blacks, Latinos, Orientals—they had just been moving in after the war, in '48. So I went to a place where you had all these races. I mean, my teammates, my playmates were Japanese, Chinese, Filipinos, whites, other blacks, the Latinos. I went to a place where you constantly heard different languages, kids going home to eat different kinds of dishes, talking about different things in school together. If I had been sent to Watts, where you had a total black ghetto, maybe the other thing could have happened to me. If I had gone to Harlem, it could have happened. If I had gone to the South Side of Chicago, it could have happened. But I was lucky.

Then, after that, I went into the army, and when I came back, I came back to metropolitan San Francisco, a completely integrated society. At the time I started writing, really getting serious about writing, it was the Beat era. All the races—again—shared all kinds of ideas. You'd go into these nightclubs and hear all these different readings of poetry and prose, with jazz in the background. You ran into all these different things. Not that I was influenced by the beat stuff, the Kerouacs and all these kinds of guys. I thought they were all crazy in the first place. But I didn't mind being there to see what they were doing. I sat back and watched it.

To get back to the black influence, many of the young black writers, even my age and younger ones, were influenced by the most successful of black novels, and that was Richard Wright's *Native Son*. They all tried to imitate this kind of urban thing. I was not urban. I tried to play that urban stuff for about two years after I went to California. If anybody asked me where I came from, I'd say, "Oh, I came from New Orleans." When they'd say name the street you lived on, I'd say, "Canal Street." Everybody knew it was a damned lie. Finally I realized, hey, man, you gotta be what you are. So I thought, well, this is what I am. This is all I am. *Native Son* would not have had an influence on me, had I read it. It's urban, Chicago. It was not a part of my experience. I didn't know a thing about urban life. If I had come from New Orleans, if I had been there and seen the violence, seen the [French] Quarter, seen that kind of background, maybe I could have tried to write that. But I came from a place where people sat around and chewed sugarcane and roasted sweet potatoes and peanuts in the ashes and sat on ditch banks and told tales and sat on porches and went into the swamps and went into the fields—that's what I came from.

MG: The big city was New Roads.

GAINES: New Roads was the big city. I'd go there to see—I don't think there was a stoplight there—just to see a light. All that made a big difference. I think if I'd gone to the eastern part of the country, I probably would have gone into playwriting. My earlier teachers said I had that sense of place, using small areas and then a lot of dialogue, and that my whole scenes were place and then dialogue, place and dialogue. My movement was limited when I was a kid growing up. I mean I had the fields and things like that, but we were limited to the quarters as our living place. Just about everything we did was limited to the quarters. We went to the big city of New Roads every so often on Friday nights to see cowboy movies, but everything else was limited to that small area.

3

Fictional Characters and
Real People

CW: You've written a novel [*A Gathering of Old Men*] about the old men now, and in nearly everything you've written, there are old people who are extremely important.

GAINES: Oh, yes, yes. I was raised by people like that. I was very close to the old people when I was a kid growing up, because I was one of the brighter kids on this plantation. Many of these people had not gone to school at all—they had no chance of going to school—so I had to do a lot of their writing and their reading for them. I suppose I learned very early in life that they were very intelligent people. I must have learned that from them at that time. Yet they were illiterate; they could not read or write. And I learned that I had to respect them. Whether they were your family or not, you respected people. They trusted and they loved me. For example, Reese. By the time I started talking to Reese again, I had been gone from Louisiana maybe thirty years—twenty-five, thirty years—but there was a closeness. He had known my grandparents' grandparents, so that connection was there. And my aunt, Augustine Jefferson, who raised me, who was crippled—and I've said this many times before—that since she couldn't travel, the old people used to come around our place all the time to talk to her, and I was there, and I had a chance to be around them. So I was very close to the old ones.

MG: There are a number of old women characters who play prominent roles in your fiction. There's the mother-in-law in "A Long Day in November," who is an aggressive kind of older woman, and you have the older women and how they are dealing with mortality and aging in "Just Like a Tree," which may be where you do the most with the idea of aging. These older women seem to be much more in control of their world than do, say, the older men in *A Gathering of Old Men*, at least up to the time the story starts. Do you see the process of aging, the effects of aging, as different for women than for men?

GAINES: The only way I can answer this is by saying I was raised by older women as a child. My stepfather . . . was not at home; he was in the merchant marine all the time. I was the oldest child around the place, and you must remember that I left when I was fifteen years old, so until that time I was around the house a lot. Of course, I went into the fields and into the swamp, where the men worked, but the relationships with the men were quite tenuous. I worked around them, but I went back home. I came in contact with them, meeting them in the quarters, or riding in a car or a wagon with them, talking to them, and working in the fields around there, but it was not as strong a relationship as the one at the house with my aunt and the people who visited her. I was around older women much more than I was around the men who came around the place where I lived.

Yet there were times when men did talk, and I think I became closer to older men when I started coming back to the South and wanted to write about things. And it seemed the older men were the ones who were there, the ones who had survived. So, in *A Gathering of Old Men*, I could bring them into the story much better than I could earlier, because when I lived in the South earlier, they were not as close to me as were the older women. As I said, our relationship was a tenuous one. I saw them, and we talked and we did things, but they were not in the household. I didn't have an older uncle or [a] grandfather in the household. My father and mother were separated, and my stepfather was in the merchant marine, so he wasn't there in the household. I was the oldest son, and I had to do the physical work. I had to be the man in the house at an early age.

The older men are not in the earlier books because they were not in my life as a child. They were there, but they were not in the immediate surroundings. They were there at a distance, like I can see my neighbors out here. We saw each other. We'd meet and we'd talk a little bit, but the eating together and the conversations at the fireplace were not there. Conversations out on the road or on the river, in the fields or in the swamps, could be there, but the contact at the house was not there. All that shows the impact the older women had on my young life, and maybe that is the reason the older men did not come in as strong figures in the earlier books and stories.

MG: The point is not to say that one group was in fact strong and the other one was not, but instead that, for whatever reasons, the women seem to feel more secure than the men do.

GAINES: I can see that, too, because the women in their work did not come in conflict with the outer world as much as the men did in their work. The men competed with the white man, and there could be conflicts there. The black man competed with the white man as sharecropper and when he went into town, whereas the black woman very seldom competed. She was just a worker there. She was a worker in the big house, and she was a worker in the field. She did not have to—as I have [shown the men doing] in A Gathering of Old Men—compete [by] racing to the derrick to unload the sugarcane, or go into the cotton gin to unload the cotton. In my world, it was not a competitive thing between the black woman and that outer world. She just did what she was supposed to do.

MG: So she had the sense that this place in the quarters was hers. She could operate there fairly securely.

GAINES: I don't know how secure her position was. I guess she had to suffer and work.

CW: Obviously we're talking about security here in relative terms, but your talking about this makes me think of Catherine Carmier. Raoul is competing with the white sharecroppers. Della will be affected by that competition, even though she is not engaged in it in the same way. She also has not had the sense of defeat, or the frustration, that the men have had. And in A Gathering of Old Men, it's finally that frustration and sense of defeat all coming together, to the point at which they're not going to do that anymore.

GAINES: Well, they've reached a point in old age—at seventy years—where it doesn't make any difference anymore. Raoul is a man maybe in his fifties. Now, when these other men were fifty, they would not compete like this. That's what Mapes keeps telling them, saying, "Hey, you would not have done that thirty years ago."

MG: They say it to themselves.

GAINES: Of course. So at seventy, seventy-five, and eighty, they say, "Well, what the hell am I going to live for? So I die today, what is that?" But they would not say that at fifty, not as a group. As [individuals], yes, maybe. But they would never have come together like that.

MG: In your works, you have older people who are very strong. For example, in "Just Like a Tree," we see the older person who doesn't want to be moved. In her own way, she's not defeated. Then you have the older lady in "The Sky Is Gray," the white lady, who is very helpful to the black mother and child. Miss Jane is a study in herself, and so are all the people in A Gathering of Old Men. It seems that you have so many pictures of older people dealing with old age. Do you think your books portray how you feel about aging?

GAINES: You're dealing with people who had no other world. They don't know anything else. I don't know if that has any of my own personal ideas of what it means to be old. I don't think that I would be as contented as they, if I ever get to be old—and there are times when I don't think that I will. I don't think that I could ever be as they are. The people whom you brought up—Miss Jane as well as Aunt Fe in "Just Like a Tree," the older woman in "The Sky Is Gray," or the old men in A Gathering of Old Men—these people have nothing else but that little world where they have always lived. They've lived in the same place all the time. And they've done as well for themselves and as well toward humanity as they could possibly do. Since they've never traveled, they don't know what it means to not get out of—and I can use the word trap or whatever—but not get out of that little provincial world where they've spent their lives.

MG: I see the older people in many of your works as people who are very wise about being human, who have some understanding about the whole human condition.

GAINES: I think in most cases they are, because they've settled there, and from their own observations, from a certain point, they have learned so much about the human condition. And I think if you traveled the entire world, you'd find the basic desires, the basic needs, the basic loves and hates, are common among men all over the world. Most of all, old people deal with the basic things in life, basic comfort, care for one another, communication with one another, awareness of what people are like. I think they deal with basic things. When they deal with the great philosophical ideas—no, they don't know. Or great political ideas—no, they cannot have any kind of insight into these things, the people whom you have mentioned. And most of my older people are these—older, peasantlike—who remain in one place all their lives.

MG: But they are people who have learned a lot from simply having lived.

GAINES: Right. Through life. Through observation of things around them. Not having read books—they don't read books—but just seeing life and hearing about things, through their own lives.

MG: I think that in your books you get away from the stereotype that old people are sort of all alike, because you have such strong older characters who are so different.

GAINES: Because all the old people I knew *were* different. For example, you went out there and saw Pete and Reese, and those two men were as different as anything. They were as different as any two men could be. They both were very proud men. They both were men of strong character. But where Pete had lived a sort of hellish life—I mean he had a lot of women and a lot of children, probably a hundred grandchildren—Reese was much more monogamous. I think he had two wives. He went to church, believed in the church—and you couldn't catch Pete going near a church. He would go by, around about, to get where he wanted, before he'd go in a church. They were different kinds of men. I know Madame Bayonne, in *Catherine Carmier*, was a very, very dignified person. She'd just sort of sit there all the time. She'd been a schoolteacher, a little old elementary schoolteacher, but she was a very intelligent person, and I based her on a lady I knew, whom I called Cousin Louise. She was the wife of my grandmother's stepfather.

I've never known anyone as strong as my aunt, physically and, to me, morally as strong as my aunt, who never walked a day in her life. A different person from anyone else I've known all my life. So I've known some very strong people. And they were physically strong as well as morally strong, and they had their own characteristics. They had dislikes, they had their hatreds, they had their likes, they raised their children differently.

MG: The common concept is that when older people get eccentric, it's because of old age, when quite often they were like that all their lives. It also seems true of your characters that they are not stereotyped, that there are older characters who do change, and there are other characters who never change.

GAINES: Oh, yes, I have stereotypes in my books. For example, Bishop in *Of Love and Dust* is a stereotyped character, but then I have someone to counter it, like in Marcus. Marcus is going to counter Bishop; he's just the opposite of whatever you think when you say [about Bishop], "There's a stereotype black." You get somebody like Marcus who'll say, "Wait a minute, pardner. We're not all like this guy, and before I'll be like this guy, I'll be dead. I'll die first."

MG: That's what I was trying to get to. I wanted something to characterize the older people, and they're very, very different, like the mother-in-law in "A Long Day in November."

GAINES: Oh, yeah. I wanted a comic figure. That's what I wanted all the time in her.

MG: This all seems connected to how you portray men and women in general, and to how you show the black man in relation to women, and how other writers—for example, Alice Walker and Nto-zake Shange—show that relationship. Some critics have criticized you for being too kind to the black man, and in some other writers' works, especially some black female writers, there are no redeeming qualities in the black male character. There is such a contrast, in fact, between your portrayal of these man-woman relationships and the way we see them in other black writers' works, that there is a question about how you verify that your portrayal is an accurate one—the one that some people say is too kind to the black male character.

GAINES: Those same kind of people have said I'm too kind to white characters, and others have said I make my black heroes too nice, too. But I've lived with and seen the actions of these men. I think I know more about the black male because I'm male myself. I know something about his dreams. I listened to them when I was a kid grow-ing up, I've drunk with him, I've been in the army and in athletics—

I know what men dream about. All men dream about certain things. All men have hopes, and all men brutalize other things near them, at home, when they cannot fulfill those hopes. I read Joyce's Dublin stories, and I see the same sort of thing. I read this story, "The Informer," that was made into a great film about how these men are afraid of the Black and Tan—the British—and how they treated other people around them. You'll find that, among men, the more brutalized they are, the more they brutalize other people. I remember reading Faulkner's "Dry September," where they come from this lynch mob and this guy comes home to his wife. His wife says something to him, and he wants to beat her up. It's just continual brutalization of one thing after another. The lynching was not even enough for him to get rid of all the aggressiveness or hatred or whatever it was that drove him to participate in the lynching. He comes back to the house and he continues it at home.

But then there's the other side of things as well. It's not only one side. I never look at things just one way. In my writing about black males, I've known the cowards, I've known the men who would take chances—men who, if they were given the equal chance, would be as brave as any man. We can see that in athletics. We can see that in reading about soldiers, guys fighting in Vietnam or the Second World War: that men, given an equal chance, will say, "OK, I'm a man," and he does his job as well as anyone else does. This is complicated stuff.

MG: There's a lot of violence in some of your stories—for example, the fight at the house party in *Of Love and Dust*. But it seems to be more directed toward other men, and not toward the women. Do you think other writers have a false image, that they're showing too much of that [violence of men toward women]?

GAINES: I don't know, because I think if they did not have the violence there, they'd have the violence someplace else. If the violence were not exercised at that particular party, it would have been exercised somewhere else. But what brought on this violence? What brought on this thing at that particular time at the house party? Number one, it's hot. Number two, the beer is warm. Number three, there's nothing else to do. Number four, Marcus is there, and he's looking for a fight because he couldn't get with this woman he wants. The woman cannot be with him, because of other reasons. She's told him, "Get away from me," because she belongs to Sidney Bonbon. It's not just a guy going out there and beating up on a woman or beating up on somebody else because of nothing else. You have to look at what causes these things. You can't say a guy beating up on a person out there is just beating up on someone. What brought him to beat up on that person, or to act the way he's doing? This is the kind of thing that I try to figure out.

CW: Anyone who tries to write fiction has a store of lines from other writers that he wishes he had written. One of yours that I wish I had done is in "Bloodline," when you're talking about the old woman, Amalia, walking, and her husband, Felix, says, "Even walking downhill looked like an incline." It's the perfect image of an old person walking downhill.

GAINES: I know another thing you told me one time. You said—in *A Gathering of Old Men*, where Candy meets the old men—and in the story I wrote, "where the gate used to be," and you said, God, that's a good one. Where the gate used to be. You know these old country places, and there was a gate there at one time. Like twenty-five years ago, there was a gate out there. That's where the gate used to be, you know.

MG: There's another thing I wanted to touch on, and it's another line here, that line in *A Gathering of Old Men* where Fix's friend says, "I'm an old man." He says, "I don't know what's right and wrong anymore." It seems like, in that novel particularly, the older Cajun men become confused by things.

GAINES: Well, I mean, the old men become confused. Of course he would say something like that. You know, he says, twenty-five, thirty years ago, I'd ride with you, but today I'm old. We're all old. I don't know what it means to be liberal today or conservative. I don't know what it means to be right-wing or left-wing. I don't know what it means to go defend the white woman's honor or to go to war anymore. I don't know what is right and wrong. The older you get, the more you realize, I don't know what right and wrong are anymore.

MG: But, at least, in *A Gathering of Old Men*, the black men come to a better understanding of what's right and wrong.

GAINES: I think if it was to gather for a certain thing—see, this thing is a gathering for something that they have always felt, probably felt: "Hey, we are doing this because we have an advantage to do these kinds of things. We *can* do this." I think tomorrow I'd give you a better explanation, if we were doing this tomorrow.

CW: There's a kind of a general need to do it in order to keep their advantage.

GAINES: Right, true, there you go. Where the old men have never done this—I mean, they've never stood up for anything. So suddenly they say, hey, we have to stand up. We have to do something. That's the only difference there. We have never done anything. These old men over here are saying, "Well, I don't know if that's right anymore." And probably when they went riding with Fix thirty years ago, they probably thought to themselves, "Are we really doing the right thing? Are we doing the right thing now?" And now they would admit, "Hey, you know, I've been thinking I don't know if that's right anymore." And that's what I think [Fix's friend is] saying.

MG: It's really sort of a mob mentality that makes the younger ones do this. They get just sort of embroiled, when to the old men, that's not enough to make them act.

GAINES: Right. These men are tired. They're just sort of sitting there with nice white shirts, stiff white shirts, and they're stiff in their chairs, listening to what's going on around, and their arms, they don't have all the blood in them anymore, you can see their veins—I didn't describe all of that—"I don't know if this is right. I don't know what is right anymore. I don't know what is wrong anymore. I don't know what we're doing anymore." I got a nice letter from a guy from Hawaii just the other day, and he said the line he likes [best] in the entire book is when Dirty Red is lying beside Charlie in the fight scene at the very end, and Charlie says to Dirty Red, he says, "Dirty, life is so sweet when you know you ain't no more coward." That guy says, "I would get that line and I would have it printed in every school, from elementary school to university, in the country." He says it's a fantastic line because it took a man like Charlie three hundred years to speak that line. He said, "If you ever get to Hawaii, visit me."

MG: One other thing about old people: What do you think

makes some old people able to change and adjust and others not able to do it?

GAINES: Maybe genes, or whatever. I don't know if genes do that. I was listening, I was reading something about the Italians, and there was an interview with Italians, and Tony Bennett says the reason Italians sing so well is it's in their genes. Well, I don't know if I agree with that sort of thing, you know, because they do other things, too, you know. I don't know. Maybe it's characteristic of people, or some people: it's possible to change sometimes, somewhere. And others just refuse to do that. I really don't know what makes people change. I have no idea what causes people to change.

MG: I think that in your books you show that it's not something that you can pinpoint, because you have the black characters who change and the white characters who change and those who don't. It's very much an individual thing and sometimes not predictable.

GAINES: There you go. There you go. It's an individual thing. I wouldn't dare say it's racial or of certain areas or certain pressures. I don't give a damn what you're doing. You can drop that nuclear bomb here today, you're going to find some people who will come together and say, hey, we better do something. And you'll have some sons of bitches who'll say, I'm not getting out, I'm still going to be what I am. They won't change.

I don't know what causes change. I don't know if, had I not left the South at the time I did—and I think I left at the best time of my life. I left after I'd learned so much. Because I had learned a hell of a lot in my fifteen and a half years. I had learned the small towns, how you had to survive going into the small towns. I had learned about going into swamps and pulling the end of a saw, drove the axe that split the logs. I had learned to go into the fields and work. I had learned to fish. I had learned so many things, but I left at a time, at an earlier age, where I had not been crushed. I had not become bitter like so many of the younger kids whom I left here [had become] when I came back and began to see them ten years later. They didn't care anymore about anything.

I know that going away educated me, but I don't know that it made a change in my character. Maybe my character was already developed from the kind of responsibilities I had to take as a child, as a small child. Maybe my character was developed from that point. And maybe I would've become what I am today—maybe not a writer, you know—and maybe not. Maybe I would've become just bitter. Maybe I would've become a teacher and then blamed the world for everyone except myself. Say: "OK, I'm nothing but a teacher, and I don't want to be a teacher, I want to be something else. I want to be a writer, but because I could not get a chance to be taught this other thing, I'm going to hate the world for it." I don't know but that could've happened to me. So I have no idea what really changes people. Maybe it's some little thing that happens in life, moving or— [Pause]

MG: One time you said it was the little things—and you used the example of the girl putting on lipstick—those little things in life are going to change the direction of your life one way or another. Once it's there, you can't really go back and undo it. Do you believe that that's in general true, that there are little things that happen that we can't control or predict?

GAINES: Oh, yes. I believe the old thing, you know, because of the nail the shoe was lost, because of the shoe the horse got crippled, and because of that the war is lost. I know Tolstoy once said that no matter how well you prepare for war—everything is ready, everything is set—but if that horse neighs at the wrong time, whinnies at the wrong time, the whole thing is thrown off, because the enemy knows you're there, waiting, and then everything falls apart.

CW: In the title story, "Bloodline," you've got four old people there. You've got Frank, who's the white owner of the plantation, who's very perceptive, and you treat him very sympathetically at the same time that he represents something that you obviously feel has to change. He's aware of the need for the change; it's just that he's unable himself to implement it. It's something that has to come after him.

GAINES: Right. It's something like Marshall in *A Gathering of Old Men*. He says: "I didn't intend any of this stuff, and I can't be bothered with any of it. You guys do what you want to do."

CW: And Frank, to a certain extent, takes that view. And there's Felix, who's just trying to get through, and he wishes that Copper wouldn't come and cause this commotion, but he can't betray Copper either. [Copper is the young mulatto in "Bloodline" who has been driven into madness because his white father has denied him.] He understands where Copper is coming from. And Amalia is torn between them. And there's the old butler, who is the kind of comic, cowardly figure. I was reading that story this morning, and I wondered about something. Looking at the old people, I know you see things in their world that needed to be changed. Do you also see things in that world that you wish could be retained?

GAINES: Yes. I would think a faith in God is one thing. I think that if we could change the whole world and keep the land is another thing. Change things yet keep the relationship is another thing. But it seems that when we change, we plow the whole damned thing up. We destroy the barn to get rid of the mouse in the barn. The damned rat in the barn has to be gotten rid of, and sometimes it seems we just have to burn the whole barn down to get rid of it. It's too bad that we do that because we don't know any other way to get rid of the rat in the barn. It's the same thing with Mapes in *A Gathering of Old Men*. Mapes, in the beginning, doesn't know any other way to get information than to come and beat up people. But then the story changes, and because Mapes is such a central character, the story has to change, and he realizes that, hey, this is not the way to do it. In a lot of these other cases, it just so happens that we destroy everything before the changes. For example, Aunt Fe dies at the end of "Just Like a Tree," before the bombings stop. If the bombings stopped before, she could have lived. But the bombings were not going to stop before, so she had to die before the bombings stopped. And before they moved her out, she had to die.

So there are certain things that, yes, I do want retained, I want kept. However, we have not reached a point yet in our lives of knowing how to keep this and make the changes, too. We don't know how to keep the nice little rural church houses, rural schools. We don't know how to keep nice mom-and-pop restaurants anymore, because once we had—and we had to have—desegregation, once we changed all these things, then came hamburger joints. But, damn it, we had to change those things, and then Taco Bell and hamburger joints and Kentucky Fried Chicken and freeways and all this stuff came on afterwards. But it's too bad we could not have some intelligent man who said, "Let's change this shit, let's change this stuff, but let's keep some of the things we have had that we all want."

I go to a little place over there on Twelfth Street right now, and it's called Creole Lunch House, and there are more whites in there than there are blacks. Yet it's a black place. Those guys have suits on, white shirts and ties. They want to be able to go to this place. And twenty years ago, twenty-five years ago, they were not going there. So this is one of the things that this black woman has sort of kept going. With all the other changes, this thing is still going on. Where twenty-five years ago those white guys could not have gone there, and there's a black couple sitting over here, there's two or three white girls sitting over there eating, there are two or three black girls sitting over there, and there are only about five or six tables in that place. These are the kinds of things I think of when you ask would you like to retain anything. Yes, I'd like to retain those kinds of things. Keep them there, so I don't have to go to Kentucky Fried Chicken to eat some chicken. I don't want that. I can go over there and get some red beans and rice and something else, you know, and sit around there and talk with people whom I care to be around. Yes, these are the kinds of things I'd like to see retained. However, unfortunately, we plow up—we destroy—everything once we need to make changes. We destroy it. We kill. We murder things.

CW: And you do that so well in the "Bloodline" story, with Frank and Felix both hearing those tractors coming, and the images of them tearing down the trees and tearing up the graves and rooting up everything. Frank knows that once he dies, his niece is going to come in and wipe them all out, just as you have said you fear is going to happen to those who are left now on the plantation where you grew up.

GAINES: I know one of the present owners very well. As a matter of fact, she wrote me a beautiful Christmas card—I have it around the place. She said, "You know, Ernie, the time will come when the only memory we'll have of this place will be in your books." And I'll keep that Christmas card forever. She has always said that they will never touch that cemetery as long as she's around. There were about twenty to twenty-five houses there at one time. In five or ten years, I'm sure this place will have no more people living there.

CW: Not everybody in your books looks at the old people the same way. In "Three Men," for example, your narrator says: "That's how old people is. They always want you to do something they never did when they was young." So there is that conflict between old and young.

GAINES: But I think you have that among young people, though—and especially with someone who is as rebellious as this young guy I have in that book. You have to understand what he's telling him to do. Look at what Munford is telling Proctor to do. He's telling Proctor to be a man. Proctor says: "Oh, wait a while, sport. You were no man. You could not be. Now you're telling me to be something? You're just like the rest of these old people around here, something you never could be. Now you want me to be it. Aw, no, don't tell me what to be." Until that young kid comes in on the scene. That's when he realizes he has to be a man. He says: "You old people are not going to come around here and tell me how to live. You never lived. You never stood up for anything. You never stood your ground. That's why you're here [in jail]. That's why you're here now, so don't tell me all of that." So you have to get the character who puts down the old people.

CW: This character and the young man in the waiting room in "The Sky Is Gray" are your characters who are the most rebellious. They also deny explicitly any religious faith, any faith in God. Why?

GAINES: Because I think that is characteristic of certain blacks in this country. You know, we like to think about blacks doing all this [Gaines claps his hands and makes a little singing sound as if to mimic the stereotype of the happy black at a revival]. But we don't think about all those people who don't go to church. We ought to think about these guys who say: "I'm going to be a gambler. I love gambling. I love doing this, because that stuff out there [the church] isn't doing a damned thing for anybody." Now, there are guys who think that way in all races, so you have these kinds of guys, too. And they say, "I'm not going along with the game." They are all rebels. These guys all say, "Hell, why should I go along with anything society says, when

I've never been given a chance to participate in society?" And others are always going to say that tomorrow is going to be a better day, tomorrow *has* to be a better day. You have those who say tomorrow will be a better day, so I'm going to be strong today, so I can be stronger tomorrow. You have the others who say the hell with it all, I'll never have a chance. And then you have the others who say I'm a defeatist. Now that's what "Three Men" is all about. You have the defeatist . . . like Hattie—the effeminate, the homosexual type thing, you know, just given up: I'll be whatever the world wants me to be. I will not try to be a man. Munford has gone just the opposite way: if anything gets in my way, I'm going to knock it over with a gun, or with an axe, or with anything. And then you have this other guy, Proctor, who says, "I just want to exist, and I don't give a damn how I exist"—until he realizes the only thing is, when you can give up [indifference to] life, then you become something.

So you're going to have that among any group. You will have this rebellion against authority. You have these kids, you know: I'll stick a goddamned needle in my arm, I'll sniff coke, to hell with anybody telling me what to do. Can I get a job tomorrow? Can I move here tomorrow? Can I live here tomorrow? Can I be recognized tomorrow? Well, if I can't, to hell with it. I'll take coke, or I'll use any kind of profanity, I don't give a damn. You have that. You have those kinds. Then you have that other one who says, hey, I'm going to try a little bit harder, try just a little bit harder to do these things right, and maybe it'll be better tomorrow for me.

CW: With Proctor, you do a neat little turn at the end, because he pleads with the other, younger boy to pray for him. He can't believe, but he wants to know that somebody back there does.

GAINES: Yes, yes. That's the only way he could survive. He realized that he couldn't survive the kind of torture, or the kind of thing he probably [would have to] go through.

CW: He still doesn't know, even at the end. He still doesn't know whether he's going to make it or not.

GAINES: Right. Yes. He does not know. He's looking out there, you know, when he's lying on the bunk, and he's trying to find a star. He had concentrated on one star a long time, and then something broke the concentration. And he looked back out there again and said: "Now which one was mine? And I won't cheat. I have to get mine, because if I cheat, I'm cheating me now." So he's going back to him [the younger man] and saying, man, this is the only way you're going to survive this world. That's the existentialist thing I was reading at that time, you know. If I cheat on one star out there, I've cheated, and I will not cheat myself. I cannot cheat myself. I must be a man to believe in one star out there, you know, just to believe that's the star I chose for my direction in life. I must concentrate on that. I must live with that because I chose that. That's my way of living.

CW: When did you read *The Sound and the Fury* in relation to writing this story?

GAINES: Oh, much earlier. I read *The Sound and the Fury* before I wrote "A Long Day in November," and that was in the fifties. "Three Men" I didn't write until '64 or something like that, six years later.

CW: You do something in that story that made me ask that question. Remember in the scene in which Quentin Compson is on his way home and he's on the train and he sees the black man on the mule and he makes the remark that "the nigger is the obverse reflection of the white man," the other side of the coin. And you do that in here. Munford tells Proctor that the white man "by looking at us he knows what he is not." And that's the "obverse reflection" idea. The white man defines himself by knowing what he isn't. How is that different from the way the black man defines himself?

GAINES: That's a big question you ask me there all of a sudden, and I don't know how I'd go about answering that question. The thing you asked me is, What is man and how does the black man go about defining himself?

CW: Yes.

GAINES: Yeah, well I'd have to think on that, really a lot.

CW: OK, do that. We'll come back later and deal with it again another time.

GAINES: That is a good question, and I know I've thought about it many times. I know I've written things about it many times. How do I identify myself? No matter what I think of myself, I am caught up in a certain culture that says you're not this or you're not that. I'm kind of caught up in that. And I must find that thing in me, just like that star that Proctor finds. I must find that thing in me and say, OK, you are that. And damn it, that's what you are. You follow this code of life, which I think I do as a man, as a writer. That's how I define myself.

I know who I am. I know that I was born in Pointe Coupée Parish. I know that I grew up on a plantation. I know about the old people around me who sacrificed everything for me to educate me. I know that I have written books. I know that my books have been translated into many languages. I know all these things about myself. I know that I care for my family. I know that I care for my friends. I know that I don't give a damn for my enemies. I know that I don't judge all whites as my enemies; I don't judge them as my friends, either. I know I have white friends. I don't say that all blacks are my friends, because I don't have too many black friends here in the city of Lafayette. I say I must go on and do my work, I must earn my living, I must do my teaching, yet communicate with my friends, be with my friends, and all this sort of thing.

I think your question was how do you define, how do you define a black man just by his— [Pause]

CW: If the white man in this culture that you're writing about— whether or not it works today, because of changes, would be something else we would have to explore—but in that culture, if the white man defines himself because he can look at the black man and say, well, I'm not that.

GAINES: I cannot do the same thing, of course. No, no—I *won't* do the same thing.

CW: So how does the black man define himself in that culture?

GAINES: Well, I think I was trying to explain in my way how I do it. I will not say, "I know who I am because I don't want to be *that*." I don't say things like that. I take a much more positive attitude, I think, about the thing.

CW: In "Three Men," that's what Proctor is doing. That's what Copper is doing in "Bloodline," even if Copper may truly be crazy.

GAINES: He is.

CW: That's what he's doing at the same time in his own mad way.

GAINES: Well, Copper, Marcus, and Proctor, they're almost the same character. They're the kind of character I was focusing on at that time. Part of my brain was working in that one direction.

MG: It's a type of white man in that culture. It's not saying particularly that every white man defines himself like that.

GAINES: Right, because there's the young white deputy in there, and Proctor gets along with him quite well.

CW: In fact, the young deputy warns Proctor about the mean, older deputy, T. J.

GAINES: He warns him against T. J. He says here are some cigarettes, and just cool it. Don't provoke these people. And Proctor talks about a young guy who used to play baseball with him all the time. He wanted to play in the outfield—because he liked to run—and be around with them all the time.

CW: And bought them Cokes when it was over.

GAINES: Right. So he understood those kinds of people. I think he understood T. J. as just being a vicious person, whereas Munford was around long enough—an old guy, a con—long enough to come in and out of that prison, [and he] told us exactly what T. J. was all about.

CW: I find it interesting that you said the three—Copper, Proctor Lewis, and Marcus—that you see them as basically the same person. At the same time, they're very different. So, first, why Copper's madness?

GAINES: Well, maybe because I had read *Lear*. [Laughter] Because I had read *King Lear* and *Don Quixote* could be two reasons why he's mad. I think something probably happened. I think he says something about—that he realized one day that not only blacks died in electric chairs. I think Copper says that somewhere. He had to clean the chair and found a single brown hair, and he says, "Goddamn it, these people are killing their own children now." That might have been the thing that clicked. Maybe he could have been just angry, but then he says: "I know I don't have a chance now. If they burn their own kids up, I know I don't have a chance in this world." That and, possibly, I think that he mentions that his stepfather never did care for him. I think that's one of the other things. He's just thrust out there. He's just put out there, and nobody cared anything in the world about his life. And Copper is, of course, as much white as he is black, and he's caught up in a world where he's not any part of the world. He's betwixt and between, where he cannot go one way or the other. It keeps pulling him apart. Jim Bon in Faulkner's *Absalom, Absalom!*— that sort of thing. He says, OK, where do I fit into this whole scene? And when you don't find a place to fit in, madness can easily happen to you.

MG: It's important to be able to make that human connection and have a sense of one's own place and that one has a relationship with others.

GAINES: When he talks about his soldiers, he's talking about all kinds of people. He says, you think I'm talking only about myself, but there are other people who have been denied a place in the sun. I'm not only talking about me now. I'm not only talking about blacks now. But I'm talking about all of those who have been denied that sort of thing. And that's the army in his madness who he envisioned will join him. I wasn't being facetious awhile ago when I said *Lear* and *Don Quixote.* When Quixote was attacking those damned windmills—it's that sort of thing. These are the kinds of things you pick up, the kinds of things you learn when you read. That's why I tell my students to read so much. They say, What do I want to read *Madame Bovary* for? I say just read it anyhow, because if you find one line in it, you'll treasure it.

CW: You'll never know when you'll use it.

GAINES: You never do. You never know when you'll use anything.

MG: You once said that you didn't want to write a sequel to *The Autobiography of Miss Jane Pittman*, but you also recognized that *In My Father's House* was not the book your audience expected. Nevertheless, it was the book you had to write. Is there any reason why?

GAINES: Well, I think it was the book I had tried to write many, many times before, and I think I had reached a point where I just had to—it stuck in my craw, and I just had to get it done. I think it was the book I wanted to write after I finished *Catherine Carmier,* and I never could finish it. I never could write it. I could write a draft, and it didn't feel right. Then I'd put it aside, and I'd write something else. I wrote *Of Love and Dust*, and I wrote the *Bloodline* stories. And I tried to write it again, and it just never did go away. And finally, after I wrote *Miss Jane Pittman*, I had to go back to it again. I figured that if it was something that was in me, something I wanted to do since *Catherine Carmier*, and something I kept going back to and going back to, it was going to be there until I finally got rid of it, and then I would be free to do other things.

So I had to get rid of it. I had to excise, or exorcise, it before I was free to do other things—although I've been least satisfied with that book than any other that I've written. I've never been able to just read it out in public as I've done with the others, *A Gathering of Old Men, Miss Jane Pittman, Of Love and Dust*, and whatever. Those books I can read anytime, but *In My Father's House* I could never read in public, never wanted to read. It was just something I had to get done. I got it done, and that's all over with, and I'm not terribly, terribly happy with it. But I feel, in a way, it's a different book. It's a good book. I feel I have a good dramatic situation there. At the same time, I don't know if it is a successfully readable book, one you can go back to and go back to. Different people say different books are their favorites. I don't know of anyone who says *Miss Jane* is their favorite, unless they haven't read anything else. And yet it's the most popular book.

CW: You wrote it [*In My Father's House*], put it away, came back to it, and wrote it again, several times. Why such urgency to do that book? Where did that urgency come from?

GAINES: Oh, I don't know. It's not a typical story, but I think it's a story—I don't want to say a typical story, because I don't want to say every child is looking to destroy his father and all that Oedipus bull. I don't believe in that. I wanted to write in some way something based on Greek tragedy. I wanted to write of a great man falling and then, some kind of way, coming back. I want to show father-son separated. As I've always said, father-son separated on the slave blocks when they came here, and they've never really come together since then, in the last three hundred years. The system has not allowed it.

Now the system allows father or son to become Christianized, to go to church and to have the power and strength to do certain things. For example, the father has the power, when he's converted to Christianity, to lead. All of a sudden he's a very strong man, a powerful man, and yet that same strength fails. That's why he questions God: "Now wait a minute. You gave me the strength to do these things that fall under the democratic system of government, where men have the right to pursue happiness, but when I come to the thing I want, and that is to bring my son to me, you fail me." And this is what I was trying to do, and I still haven't done it. That's why I keep writing stories about fathers and sons: because I still haven't done it. I think this is what I was trying to do all the time. I had done it in a comic way in "A Long Day in November."

CW: Do you think there's something like that working in the relationship between Jim and Marcus in *Of Love and Dust*?

GAINES: Well, it could be. Who brought that point up about Raoul and Jackson in *Catherine Carmier*? They said, here's the son Raoul always wanted, and here's the father Jackson always wanted, and yet when they come together, they must battle.

CW: There's also a very different God in *In My Father's House* from the one in *Of Love and Dust*.

GAINES: That's right. Well, you're dealing with Jim and Marcus. Jim, I suppose, thought He'd forgotten about man, but apparently He had not.

CW: Frank Shelton remarks that Phillip Martin and other black male characters lack a certain kind of maturity that the women in their lives seem to have. That even here—that not only as you do in the other stories, where the old women have so much strength—but the women the same age as Phillip Martin seem to have a better awareness of what's going on and how to deal with the world than he does.[1]

GAINES: I don't know. I think at that particular time, you thought about only one thing, and that was how to get a drink of water, how to get demonstrations organized, and that was the thing that was done. And I'm very sure that a lot of people who led these

---

1. Frank W. Shelton, "*In My Father's House:* Ernest Gaines after Jane Pittman," *Southern Review*, n.s., XVII (1981), 343–44.

things were very, very brave people, and although they were very ignorant of the world, really, they knew this was what they had to do.
This was what Phillip Martin was called to do, to lead. And as for the
humanity and all the other things that make one strong and make one
whole, maybe he lacked those things. But he was strong enough to
know how to get people into stores and how to get people to the
fountain and how to get people to vote and things like this. And this
was the most important thing. If I had read that article before I wrote
the book, I would have added all those things. [Laughter] Unfortunately, I did not.

CW: The single-mindedness of purpose, then, detracts from his
wholeness.

GAINES: Of course. You concentrate so much on one thing that
there is nothing else that's important. Just like his wife is not important. Alma's not important. She says: "What you want? You want me
to go to church with you or you want me to go to bed, and that's it.
You don't involve me in anything." And that was all he wanted. "I
must get these people to vote. That's what we're supposed to do, I'm
going to do it. And I'll walk on anybody to do it." And that's how he
felt: "Now, I cannot be dealing with you on the side, but I must get
those people to vote. And that's all there is to it." And that is a weakness of man. His weakness, the reason he does not get up, is he let the
liberal decide who the heck he is. He let the liberal whites decide who
he is. They decided he was tired, and he accepted their decision without saying, "No, I'm not. This is my son." This is why he failed. This
is sort of the help he could go to to get something moving like that,
but they're the same people who kept him on his back when he wanted
to get to his son. That's part of the scheme: We can help you to get a
drink of water, we can have you sit at the counter, but we cannot help
you to understand your son or your son to understand you. Our poli-
cies are not written that way.

CW: You just said a minute ago that, again, you didn't get this
done the way you wanted to.

GAINES: I think most people feel that is my least successful
book. Not that I don't feel that it is a good book, but I just don't have
the feeling that it was ever finished.

MG: In an interview given when you had just started to work on *In My Father's House*, you said: "It's generally about the old fight between father and son type of thing. I think in this particular instance the father is looking for the son, whereas in most of my stories the theme has been the son looking for the father."[2]

GAINES: Well, the father has been absent in most of the other stories, except in "A Long Day in November."

MG: Do you think that you kept that idea of the father looking for the son?

GAINES: I think that's part of it, but as I said, I don't think I completed everything. The father is looking for the son, of course.

CW: Several have commented on the fact that, after your other works, most of them done in the first person, you went back to the omniscient point of view. Why did you shift to that omniscient point of view?

GAINES: I didn't know who to tell that story by. I had the voice of Chippo. Chippo told the story, but I had too many internal things from Phillip Martin. He's wrestling with his soul, and who could tell that except Phillip Martin? And I didn't want him to tell the story. He couldn't tell it right, unless I get one of those Molly Bloom hundred-page soliloquies, and I didn't want that sort of thing. If I rewrote that story, I'd have Chippo tell it. And Chippo would tell it to another group of people long after it's happened. The first chapter was published in a magazine, with Chippo telling it. He told the first part of it, but I realized he couldn't tell it all.

CW: You say it's not done. Is there anything specific you can put your finger on that makes you feel that way?

GAINES: No, I don't think there is, and I feel that's why I keep writing. I keep writing books because I don't think I've ever done it. In my first novel, *Catherine Carmier*, Raoul is looking for a son, and I know I failed there, because they fight and there's a separation there. And Jackson's probably looking for a father, as [is] Marcus in *Of Love and Dust*. The boy in "Three Men" and Marcus are essentially the

2. Forrest Ingram and Barbara Steinberg, "On the Verge: An Interview with Ernest J. Gaines," *New Orleans Review*, III (1973), 340.

same character, and the boy in the story screams, "Where is my father?" In *Of Love and Dust*, it's almost the same sort of thing. Marcus does not say, "Where is my father?" But hell, if he were around, Marcus probably would not be in the situation he is in now.

CW: You get the same feeling with Copper.

GAINES: Copper, of course. He's not only been deserted by the father, he's been deserted by the whole system.

CW: Copper, also, is one who has to deny any faith in anything—and in that one, more explicitly than in any other place, you link the whole notion of religion to the culture.

GAINES: Yes. You see, once your father denies you, why should you respect the religion of your father? Why should you respect the authority of your father? And God is the highest authority of everything. Once father denied me, why should I respect anything that's connected with him at all? Why should I respect that one thing that he finds the supreme thing above him? If he denies me, then I deny the supreme thing which he thinks is above all. So I deny him. If he denies me, I deny everything he thinks of as being superior. If he denies me. And this is the kind of thing—when you said, "Why do you have the rebels?" Why the rebels? Most of my rebels, one of the things they say is, where's my father?

CW: All of them. Proctor says it—

GAINES: All of them say that. Proctor says the same thing. Where is my father? You talk, but where is my father? Don't tell me to respect this thing here. Where's my father?

CW: Some of them have been left by him. For others, the father has died.

GAINES: Right. And he says: "Now, if he was here to guide me, then demand this of me. But don't tell me what to do without him, without this kind of image there for me. The image you have brought to me is an image I cannot follow." Why should Proctor respect a religion or a God that T. J. serves? Proctor says, "No way will I respect that."

CW: At the same time, in each of those cases you have somebody who at least attempts—even if he doesn't always succeed—to act as a kind of surrogate father.

GAINES: Oh yes, yes, yes. You have the same thing with Marcus and in Jim.

CW: Munford for Proctor and even Proctor for the boy.

GAINES: And even that old minister in the dentist's office ["The Sky Is Gray"] for the young nihilist. Oh yes, you do have the surrogate father come up on the scene. You have that all the time, in everything, in every book. You find that even in *In My Father's House*. He's looking for his son, you know, and the boy says, where were you? He says, well, I'm looking for you. And the young guy says, well, it's too late now. There's no reaching me now.

MG: Because it fits in so well and because I've never heard you talk about it—and if you don't want to talk about it, just say, "I don't want to talk about it"—did your own relationship with your father affect the way that you portrayed that in your books?

GAINES: I think it might have been—with my father, and not with my stepfather. Yes, yes, yes, because he was not there, and my stepfather was there.

MG: Was he never there?

GAINES: He was never there when I was a kid growing up. He was there when I was a very small child, but not after I was on my own. From the moment I was on my own, which was when I was about eight years old, he was not there. That's why I was on my own at eight. He was never there. And the stepfather came over a little bit later, and I respect him.

MG: You always indicate that you had a very close relationship with him.

GAINES: I had a very close relationship with my stepfather when he was around me, but he was in the merchant marine.

CW: He was gone, but there was always the sense that he would be back.

GAINES: Oh, yes. If I needed something, he would be there.

CW: Were you aware of where your real father was? Was he in the area?

GAINES: Well, I was in California, and he was in Louisiana.

CW: You have a period of seven years there, from eight to fifteen, where you were still in Louisiana.

GAINES: He was here. Right. He was in New Orleans, and I was in Pointe Coupée, and my stepfather was in the merchant marine then.

CW: Is your father still living?

GAINES: Yes, he's still alive, yes. But there's no connection. There's no contact. My stepfather's not alive now.

MG: But your mother is.

GAINES: Oh, my mother is. Quite alive.

4
Family and Culture

MG: What was your relationship with your mother? Did she affect how you portray old people?

GAINES: No, I never had that kind of close relationship with my mother, not as much as I did with my aunt and other older people. My mother's only about sixteen and a half years older than I, and my mother even today doesn't consider herself as being old. So when I was forming ideas about the old people, it was never my mother. I never thought about her, no way! If she thought I thought that way about her, I'd probably be thrown in jail. No way. Not my mother. I'm the oldest child. I'm closer to her, and she's like an older sister. No, my mother was never considered for one of the older people. I think the person I had in mind as my mother was in "The Sky Is Gray." That person was somewhat like her.

MG: What I see in that person is her strength. Incredibly strong.

GAINES: An incredibly strong person. Both she and my maternal grandmother were extremely strong people.

MG: In "The Sky Is Gray," the mother has a tough kind of love. She's not a mother who shows affection for the child.

GAINES: Openly.

MG: Yes, openly. In fact, the only time she touches the child is to slap him.

GAINES: Well, I would not use that phrase.

MG: She never hugs him or touches him affectionately. Was that simply not done?

GAINES: I don't know that very poor and rural-life people really show that kind of affection. I don't know that this is something that was very common among any rural people like that. Overtness is not really shown as much. I know kids have criticized me for making the mother so harsh.

MG: One of the things kids have a hard time seeing is that even whipping a child was considered a way of showing you cared—sometimes, I'm sure, it was done out of anger—it was something you had to do, a duty. But do you see the mother as essentially a loving mother?

GAINES: I don't know what you mean by a loving mother.

MG: Does she love her children?

GAINES: Oh, yes, she loves her children. Oh, yes, she loves her children. But to show that kind of thing in an overt way was something that was just not done.

CW: What was the first duty of a mother who loved her child?

GAINES: To show us how to live, to show us how to survive. My mother would show us those things. I know I was conditioned in the act of killing things for us for food. And as a small child, at the *boucheries*, I had to be one of the children to hold the pig, because at that time you did not shoot him or hit him in the head with a big sledge, but you grabbed him—the macho stuff—and threw him down and cut the throat to catch the blood for the blood pudding. And they made you hold him. I was one of the oldest boys, and I'd hold one of the legs. I'd always hold it like this [gestures as if holding it at arm's length and looking away]. Now, I could never wring a chicken's neck. If I grabbed a chicken to wring his neck, I'd drop him down and he'd start running. I could never do that. My aunt used to tell me to go out and catch a chicken. I'd catch it, but somebody else would have to kill it. My aunt would wring the neck.

As for hard work, I could do that. I went out to the swamps when I was about twelve, and I had to pull the end of a saw or take an axe to chop wood or go out to the field. So I did hard work, but as far as the killing, when it comes to the killing of animals, no. I'd go out fishing, bring in fish, and clean the fish. But actually killing something—I think I could kill something in anger, but I don't think I could ever just kill anything.

MG: One of the things about "The Sky Is Gray" is that it is so important for the students to understand the whole setting and the culture. They see the mother being harsh, but in that setting if a mother showed affection openly, especially to the young boys, it would have caused them to be regarded as sissies.

GAINES: Yes. Oh, yes. I think the mother shows tremendous consideration. She shows that same sort of attitude toward everyone she comes in contact with—for example, the old lady. The mother says, "I refuse to have your food for nothing. I'll work for what I get. I have to earn my pay." When the pimp comes in, that's another example of the kind of person she is. When she's at the place trying to eat and the pimp comes up with the "Dance, pretty?" stuff, she's ready to strike him. It's the harsh world upon her that makes her react to all things as she does. I think she loves the child, and the child is aware of that.

CW: That's why he feels the enormous swell of pride when she says, "You're a man."

GAINES: Right. And there's no time ever that he feels that he hates her. He says he's going to buy her a coat one day. And he says, "They made me understand why she made me kill the bird." That was the only way of survival.

MG: You often have used the phrase "survival with dignity" in describing your characters, and this idea seems especially evident in "The Sky Is Gray."

GAINES: Yes, that's something I got from my aunt, and from reading Hemingway, the grace-under-pressure thing—the "dignity under pressure" and "survival with dignity" are really the same thing.

MG: You have often talked about your aunt Augustine Jefferson and her influence on you. You have described her as being very strong physically and morally and very alert mentally. Though she could not walk, she cooked, washed clothes, and cared for you and your brothers and sisters. You have said that she had the *greatest* impact on your life, not only as a writer but also as a man.

GAINES: Right. Unless you include her, you can't write about me at all.

MG: Why did you first go to live with her?

GAINES: She was crippled all of her life, and she was living with us. She lived with my mother. Somebody had to look after her because she was crippled.

CW: So that's why you stayed here, to look after your aunt.

GAINES: Oh, yes.

MG: So your mother was in the house, also, when you were growing up with your aunt?

GAINES: My mother was in the house for a while. I remember my mother going with me to the dentist. I remember her going with me when I registered for the little school in New Roads, at St. Augustine. I was twelve then, and I'm pretty sure that soon after that she was gone, so that would be in '45.

MG: But until that time she lived with you.

GAINES: Well, most of the time she was in the house. She was working, and sometimes she had to work in New Orleans and other places, but most of the time until that time, she was in the house. She was there more often than not until '45.

MG: I've always pictured your aunt an older person. How old was she when she died?

GAINES: Auntie was about fifty-three, I guess. After all, you know, crawling over the floor for fifty-three years is a long, long time. I've never depicted her as an old person. I mean not as a very old person. I know I used to say the old people used to come around to be with her and talk to her, but I've never, I don't think at any time I ever gave her age.

MG: Was she one of the people who told stories?

GAINES: No. I mean, when I say "tell stories," those people didn't really tell stories. The people talked about things. My brother Lionel and I were laughing about this just yesterday. A man used to tell ghost stories all the time. That was storytelling, while sitting around burning cane shuck in the ditches in the fall. He would lie and tell stories. But with my aunt, it was much more just talking the way people would talk.

MG: Did they ever tell the Bouki and Lapin stories? Those are sort of the Louisiana versions of the Br'er Rabbit stories.

GAINES: Oh, yes. This man I was just talking about a moment ago, he told them, but he modernized them. He had rabbits, but he had tractors. And the rabbit was always messing up the tractor, knocking down the barn.

MG: Those usually had a humorous element in them.

GAINES: Oh, yes, all of this was humorous. I suppose there

was something he was trying to say in it, but it was told in a humorous way.

MG: Did you see your aunt as a very serious person, or was she one who seemed to find humor in things?

GAINES: I really don't know. I know she never complained. I know she never seemed terribly angry or bitter. So I guess she had a pretty good sense of humor about life.

MG: She didn't have a negative outlook.

GAINES: Oh, no! She was too busy raising us to have a really negative outlook. She had to make sure we survived, and she was the only adult around to do it.

MG: She was your grandmother's sister.

GAINES: No, she was my mother's father's sister.

CW: We touched on this once before lightly. Your mother left when you were about twelve or thirteen. Your father left when you were about eight?

GAINES: I guess so.

CW: Did he leave the quarters at that time and go into New Orleans?

GAINES: My father went into—you know this is one of the things I'd rather not go too deep into, family things—but my father went into service during World War II. So he was not there, and later, around '45 or so—I'm trying to get my dates right—my mother and my father must have met, and they must have just decided they were not going to be together anymore. Then my mother and my stepfather moved to California.

CW: Was your father or anyone else in your family deeply involved in religion, in the ministry?

GAINES: No. We had to go to Sunday school and things like that. They brought the Holy Sacrament to my aunt, but I don't know that my aunt was really fanatic about religion.

MG: She was Baptist also.

GAINES: We were all Baptists. I don't know that we've ever had anybody that was really crazy about it. My stepfather, of course, was Catholic. There was nobody in my family—I know my grandmother surely didn't go to church. My mother used to go, but she would go dancing as much as she would go to church. So there was nobody in that family fanatic about religion at all, and I don't think there are any of them today.

CW: You stayed in Louisiana two years after your mother moved to California. Was your father around during that time?

GAINES: No. He had already moved to New Orleans.

CW: So there was virtually no contact after he went in the service.

GAINES: None.

CW: You've told us about the hardships of your early years and the kind of background you came from. You're a person with great determination and courage and character. Where did you get that?

GAINES: That's what I don't know. I know that I had someone like my aunt. I know that. I think she had great character to survive under the obstacles that she lived under, the kinds of conditions that she had to live under. She had to have great character to survive, great will to survive with strength and with character, and maybe I got it from there. And, maybe, as a child I had to go out and take the man's role of the house. But I've known others who have done the same thing, and they did not come out to be writers, and many of them ended up in jail or other things. So I can't say that mine comes totally from that. That's why I say it's so abstract. You can't put your finger on one thing. Maybe it's a combination of things, having this love by this old crippled lady, and maybe it's something in the genes, and maybe there's something else. But I don't want to put it on the genes, and yet my family—there are nine brothers and three sisters—I think is one of the greatest families in the world. My brothers and sisters are all wonderful people. And they are highly moral people, all of us. They have good jobs. They live in good neighborhoods, they send their children to really good schools—the ones [who live] in California, not the ones in Louisiana. The ones in Louisiana do as well as they possibly can do. The older ones were born here, but the younger ones, who were born in California, also have this sort of thing in them.

CW: How many in California and Louisiana?

GAINES: There are ten of us out there and two here. [Gaines has two brothers in Louisiana, Lionel and Eugene.]

CW: How many are your real father's children and how many are your stepfather's, of the twelve?

GAINES: There are five and seven. Even my brothers here, whom I love very much, they're poor, but they have class. Now, my brother next to me [Lionel] would rather gamble than breathe air, you know. He lives to gamble, more than anything, but he's class. He doesn't beg. He wouldn't ask for anything. He would never ask me for money. My brother Eugene would ask me for money if he needed it, but Eugene is a hard worker. Right now he wants to start up a pig farm. He's a hunter and fisherman, and now he wants to raise hogs. So when my sister Lois came out, we bought a piece of land to start a hog farm.

CW: Do any of the other four have contact with your real father?

GAINES: Lionel has more than any of us. But, ah, I'm very proud of my family, with our background, both here and in California, what they've done for themselves. I don't know a family that's done more for themselves, a prouder family than our family—sometimes I think we have too much pride—a family that's accomplished as much for a group that's come from, well, you've seen where I come from. When my mother and stepfather left for California, they had nothing in their pockets, absolutely nothing. They started from the bottom. We worked and worked.

Where that kind of character comes from, I don't know. My mother had no education at all. They had no one to teach them. My stepfather was Catholic, but I don't know that religion played such a great role in the building of my character. Maybe it did. I think what religion did do was say to me you didn't have to believe in one religion or the other. Because I started off as Baptist there on False River, on that plantation, and then I went to Catholic school for three years. I had to go to the Catholic church and all that sort of thing. And it sort of told me, OK, Catholics can go to heaven, Baptists can go to heaven, so can Methodists. So I don't know where it comes from. I can easily say, OK, mine comes from knowing my aunt, living with the idea of being the kind of man she'd want me to be. But what about my younger brothers who did not know her at all?

CW: Your stepfather apparently had a very forceful personality.

GAINES: Oh, yes. Yes, definitely. But he was very seldom at home, because he was in the merchant marine. So, you know, a lot of the blame for juvenile delinquency is put on broken homes, or one parent in the house type thing, and yet there was never, at any time, more than one parent in our home. And when there was one parent, most of the time, there was no one but my aunt; neither my mother nor father was there. Where the character comes from, I don't know. It's a combination of things.

MG: In that line in "The Sky Is Gray"—"You're not a bum, you're a man"—it seems that that is something that came through in your family, whether it was from your mother or your aunt, not only for you but for all your family. She must have set some sort of standard that you could be something else. Not only are you a distinguished writer, but you're also a good, honest, likable person, and that seems to go throughout your family, and that's not true of many other writers, whose lives are chaos.

GAINES: Well, mine is not as calm as some people think it is, but there's no chaos.

MG: But we do know your values. There is the integrity and the reliability and those kinds of things.

GAINES: I got those kinds of things from the old ones and from my mother. I could tell you a story about my maternal grandmother. She died in California, and her body was brought back here. She's buried in the cemetery I showed you, the old place with all the weeds. When she was dying of cancer, a girlfriend of mine was supposed to go by and take her to the hospital one morning, a Monday morning. The girl was late getting over there, and my grandmother called a cab. She lived on the second floor—just as I live in San Francisco—and she walked down the stairs all the way to the door to wait for the cab. And while she's waiting for the cab to show up, my girlfriend came by to pick her up, to take her. My girlfriend told me how wet she was just from coming down the stairs. She had sweat so much she was soaking wet. And she helped her into the car and took her to the hospital. Not very far. She told me that as my grandmother sat down into the wheelchair, she seemed to just keep going down, going further and further down. They pushed her to the room, and six days later she was dead of cancer. But she was one of the strongest people. I mean, dying of cancer but coming down those damned stairs: if you don't get here on time, I'm going to find my way there.

And that's my attitude. It's an awful attitude to have, but I feel that same way, too. Hell, I'll walk to hell, if I couldn't depend on someone. And I think I got it from her. I know I got it from her, because everyone says I'm so much like her. We tried to put her on Medical, and she says, "I don't want any of that." For six months before she died, she was still a domestic, cleaning people's houses. She would not dare allow anybody to put her on Medical or things like that. She didn't want it. She had to stay in her own place, and she didn't want you to support her. I think she was the greatest person in the world. She had lived on that plantation where I grew up. She had been the cook there for something like thirty years. And I was sort of drawing on her experience there, in *Of Love and Dust*.

She had great strength. She said, if you're not going to be here on time, you call and let me know, and I'll do it on my own. And I think that's where I get this crazy, almost insane mania for punctuality. I think I've become a fanatic about punctuality, and I hate it, and yet I can't do a damned thing about it. People are not going to be exactly on time. If somebody tells me he's going to show up at two at my house, I don't care if it's a friend, enemy, my mother, interviewer, anybody—you're going to show up at that time. I think I'd go crazy if I'm supposed to be sitting in that electric chair at twelve midnight and they wait until twelve-fifteen—I'd die. Let's get this shit over with—those fifteen minutes—don't torture me that way. Because I set my crazy mind to something, and that is the time the thing is supposed to happen. I think that is one of my greatest faults, I really do. I honestly mean that, that I have this insane desire to have things done right and on time. Let's do it right and let's do it on time.

I learned that early. My aunt was like that. She'd say: "I want you to do this and do it right. I want you to do it at a certain time. I want you to go on and do it." If you were supposed to do something, you did it, and there was no question about it, and you did it at a certain time. But it's a fault, and it's something that will give me problems for the rest of my life, because I demand this of my friends.

MG: Charles Rowell, in an article in the *Southern Review*, talks about the importance of the quarters in all of your works. He also points out that, unlike Faulkner, you don't have the characters coming back. It's always a different quarters with different characters.[1] Do you see any time that you might want to use the same characters over? Do you have any plans to do that?

GAINES: I don't have any now, and I don't think I will in the future, because I think each book is finished as it is. I use the same parish, but Pointe Coupée Parish—and West Baton Rouge Parish, those two parishes—had at a time probably twelve or fifteen plantations. So I can be using different plantations for at least fifteen or twenty books. I can always shift around, and I put Bayonne sometimes ten miles away, twelve miles away, fifteen miles away, something like that, so I can always use the same parishes. But I don't necessarily have to use the same plantation. There are so many of them around that area. I don't know if there are twelve, but just on False River itself there were about four or five, just on one side. Then you go into West Baton Rouge Parish and there are several others back there.

MG: In *A Gathering of Old Men*, you used the place where you grew up as a setting.

GAINES: Yes. *Of Love and Dust* is the same scene, and the *Bloodline* stories, some of them, use the same scene. I have the same things in mind, but I shift trees around. I shift homes around. I can use the same place, but I can shift things around, which I do. I suppose sometimes I do describe the houses a little different if I do describe the big house. Sometimes I'll just get the effect of the house from the character within the house. You get the feeling of the house—not necessarily the physical feeling, but what it's made of—by the person who's in the house. For example, in *The Autobiography of Miss Jane Pittman*, you see quite possibly a different house than you see in *Of Love and Dust*, which is using the same house, same locale, and all that sort of

1. Charles Rowell, "The Quarters: Ernest Gaines and the Sense of Place," *Southern Review*, n.s., XXI (1985), 749.

thing, but you just get a different feeling in the house, I would think. At least that's what I tried to put in there. In most cases, I use that same house and same road. The road is gravel at one time. Lois [Gaines's sister] and I went down there the other day and, of course, it's blacktopped, as you know. It's dusty sometimes, so I can shift quarters, and if it's dust, I can say it's one quarters; if it's gravel, I can say another quarters; if it's blacktop, I can say some other quarters. If there are fewer houses, I can say such-and-such a place. I can say anything I want to. I keep changing the pieces of it.

CW: There is a correspondence between the opening of *A Gathering of Old Men*, with Snookum as the narrator, and the first story in the *Bloodline* stories, "A Long Day in November," with the child narrator.

MG: I think it also gives you the sense of that road going along the quarters, because he runs up to the big house. Another thing that many people note is a very, very strong sense of place: the use of the land, the ownership of the land, people belonging to the land but not necessarily owning it. What is your sense of the future of that land? What do you see as what's going to happen to it?

GAINES: I've no idea, no idea at all, because that land that I write about, have written about, was owned by a small number of people at that time, and most of those people are dead. And now that land has been divided into I don't know how many plots. I don't want to use it, because I'm not writing about River Lake Plantation. I'm writing about a place somewhat like the place. I'm not writing about that place. However, in answer to your question, this land is constantly changing, and I'm not keeping up with the changing of the land. Really, since my people no longer live there, I don't care for the changing of the land. I don't care what they do with it. As long as they don't destroy the cemetery where my people are buried, or the church they worshiped in. I still want to go there, but they can do whatever they want with it. I don't know what they're going to do, but I really don't care.

CW: In [the short story] "Bloodline," though, you have the image of the tractors coming, of the machines coming, and of the land changing and that old place no longer being there. You also mentioned how one person wrote to you and talked about the fact that someday your books would contain the only memories. That image suggests to me that what happens to the land has some relation to what happens to your people who were on it or who are on it. Do you see that?

GAINES: The ones who remain there. But there are so few people there now that when you say "the future of the land," I know there is no future for blacks on this place at all. What is the effect in the past? What is the effect in the present? That's one thing, but the future is 2000, and there won't be any blacks on that place in 2000.

MG: There's no real attachment—

GAINES: Oh, there's attachment to it, but there's no way that you can stay there, because you don't own it. You have no legal claim to it, and you don't know who's going to be in charge of it. And if the houses are the things that are going to keep the people on there, you can see those houses are not going to be there ten years from now. They definitely won't be there by the turn of the century. So when you ask what is the future of it, I really don't care about the place. I know Lois and I care very much about the cemetery. She was crying the other day when we went over there. She wanted to go in and visit, and we can't get in there for the weeds and all these other things. She cares very much for that, and so do I, but as far as the other thing, I'm pretty sure in the future we're going to care much more for those twelve acres that we bought in a different place altogether—because that's ours. Of course, the old people will not be buried there.

I suppose as children we loved the quarters. I mean we loved it more than the people who owned it loved it, but we were limited. See, I could love that patch of land—like Faulkner's stamp-on-the-envelope sort of thing—we could love that very much, because that's where everything was for us. But the rest of Louisiana really meant nothing to us. And this place means nothing to my younger brothers. This place means nothing in the world to them. [Pause] I'm not trying to preserve the Old South, for damned sure.

MG: Did your grandfather live on the plantation?

GAINES: He was the yardman in the big yard. My grandfather was sort of a Felix in "Bloodline." My grandfather was the yardman, and my grandmother was the housemaid and cook. But they were not the same people. My grandmother was my mother's mother. My grandfather was my father's father. They were not husband and wife. I was not as close to my grandfather as I was to the man who raised my grandmother, my mother's mother. I was closer to Papa Joe, who raised my grandmother.

MG: So both sides of your family were from the same place.

GAINES: Oh, yes, they were all from there. As Reese had said and as Pete Zeno told me, they knew my grandparents' grandparents. They knew five generations of us.

The "Big House" on River Lake Plantation, 1963
Copyright © 1978 by Ernest J. Gaines

The quarters on River Lake Plantation, mid-1960s
Copyright © 1978 by Ernest J. Gaines

The house where Gaines was born and raised, as it looked in the mid-1960s
Copyright © 1978 by Ernest J. Gaines

Gaines (third from right) with some of his people, 1968
Copyright © 1978 by Ernest J. Gaines

Walter ("Pete") Zeno, to whom *A Gathering of Old Men* is dedicated, 1968
Copyright © 1990 by Ernest J. Gaines

Canefield, River Lake Plantation
Copyright © 1978 by Ernest J. Gaines

Miss Jane Pittman's Oak, Lakeland, Pointe Coupée Parish, mid-1960s
Copyright © 1978 by Ernest J. Gaines

Two of the ladies whose talk Gaines drew upon in *The Autobiography of Miss Jane Pittman*
Copyright © 1978 by Ernest J. Gaines

Gaines at River Lake Plantation, 1987
Photo by Marcia Gaudet

The road down the quarters as it looks today
Photo by Marcia Gaudet

The quarters' oldest house, where the Big House cooks, including Gaines's grandmother, lived
Photo by Marcia Gaudet

Gaines at the site where the overseer's house once stood on
River Lake Plantation
Photo by Marcia Gaudet

The house where Reese Spooner, one of the old men, lived
Photo by Marcia Gaudet

Gaines in front of his first school and church, in the quarters
Photo by Carl Wooton

Graves in the plantation cemetery, where Gaines's people are buried
Photo by Carl Wooton

One of the older graves in the cemetery
Photo by Carl Wooton

A view of False River, where Gaines and his people fished and swam
Photo by Carl Wooton

Gaines at False River, 1987
Photo by Marcia Gaudet

5

Folklore and Ethnicity

MG: You often use folk beliefs, folk practices or traditions, folk medicine, and so on, in your writing. For example, in "A Long Day in November," there is the hoodoo lady; in *Miss Jane*, there is the reference to jumping over the broom for marriage; and in *Of Love and Dust*, Charlie Jordan uses a piece of salt meat on his foot to draw out the soreness after he stepped on a nail. How do you choose the specific items of folklore or folklife to include when you're writing?

GAINES: I don't know. I don't know, in that it depends on what the situation is. I know as a kid growing up—and it had happened to me—that in cutting your foot or sticking a thorn or a splinter in your foot, after drawing out the stick or whatever, you had this piece of salt meat tied on your foot. I don't know where they got the idea from. I know damn well I wouldn't do it today. But for the characters I'm writing about, there's nothing else for that character to do. That character would use that at that particular time, in the thirties or forties.

For example, in "The Sky Is Gray," there is the kid with a toothache. They have this guy praying over his tooth and pressing on his tooth. Of course it fails. I think it fails because they were saying two different prayers, but the damn thing fails. So they end up by going to a dentist to have the tooth extracted. If they had not gone to town, maybe I would have had something else happen. Maybe it would have been cured by the praying. I had that done to my tooth when I was a child. I also had something stuck in my foot, and salt meat was put on it. Luckily for me, I survived. Another kid died.

MG: Was all of the folklore you use in your writing learned directly from the culture, or did you get some from books?

GAINES: I didn't learn any of this from books. The only thing I learned from books was about the slave thing. Now, that I *did* learn from reading, because no one ever told me. I didn't know anyone that old to tell me that. But the salt meat thing and the praying on the tooth, I learned that from direct experience. To me, if you've been accustomed to it, it's not folklore. It's just part of your life.

MG: I think that's what makes folklore such an integral part of your work, because these things come naturally. These are the things the people would do and say and believe. When writers study a book of folklore and say, yes, I'll have them do this or that, then it becomes superimposed on the narrative. When you were growing up, did you know people who were recognized as having the power to heal or other special powers?

GAINES: At that particular time, yes. That's what "A Long Day in November" is all about. When everything else fails, you go back to the tradition, even to the point of superstition. When everything else fails, we go back to the old things and become almost primitive again.

MG: Was anyone in your family a healer?

GAINES: No, not other than the traditional herb things in the yard for making teas and that sort of thing. But there were people we would go to for certain things, and there were the hoodoo ladies.

MG: Keith Byerman, in *Fingering the Jagged Grain*, compares several of your fictional characters to characters in black folklore, such as Marcus in *Of Love and Dust* to Stagolee, the "bad man" in black folktales.[1]

GAINES: I did not consciously think of Stagolee in developing his character. I don't deal with myth and mythical characters too much. I base my characters on real people, just as Stagolee was probably based on a real character. I've seen people behave like that.

MG: Often in black folklore, when the situation is hard to handle and when there are so many negative things about it, the only way to deal with it is to see the humorous side and to have the underdog use trickster behavior to triumph over the person who is oppressing him. You seldom, if ever, use the trickster.

GAINES: I did this type of thing with Marcus in an early version of *Of Love and Dust*. I was playing games with that. It was not based

1. Keith Byerman, *Fingering the Jagged Grain: Tradition and Form in Recent Black Fiction* (Athens, Ga., 1985), 72.

on any mythical characters like Br'er Rabbit, but on real characters. It wasn't working out, though.

MG: In your fiction, there are no tricksters who triumph. The survivors are those who deal with situations with dignity, pride, and integrity, and you've often said that one of your themes is survival with dignity. Robert Hemenway has said, "Folk traditions enabled black people to survive with strength and dignity."[2] Do you think that folk beliefs and customs help people to survive with dignity?

GAINES: Yes, I would agree there, as long as they live in a certain environment, such as a plantation. If they have no access to anything else, these things do help them to survive. Chekhov said of the peasants that they would not trust anyone else, not even a doctor. They survived on their own. I went through it, and I heard about that stuff. When I began to write about it, I'd think, "Good Lord, how could they do this?" But as a child, I knew people who did these things. You say, "You're writing about folklore," but it's not folklore to me. I think damned near everything that's folklore has been done a hundred years ago and has become "folklore" to "civilized" people. But it's not folklore to the people it's happening to at the time. Hell, it's reality to the people it's happening to at the time.

MG: You're using the term *folklore* to mean only things in the past. It's used in a much broader sense by folklorists; it includes what the people believe traditionally and continue to do.

GAINES: Right. I agree with that, but when I use it in my writing, it's not that I believe it, but that my characters believe it.

MG: Through his folkore we can define the person. If we know what he believed traditionally, then we know who he is.

GAINES: Yes, and if a man has no past, he has no future.

MG: I think that's the crucial thing, when you show what the past is for these people.

GAINES: Not that you live in the past, but we must recognize it, even if we reject it. If you don't have a base, there's nothing to go on to.

2. Robert Hemenway, *Zora Neale Hurston: A Literary Biography* (Urbana, 1977), 199.

MG: In your article in *Callaloo*, "Miss Jane and I," you say: "Truth to Miss Jane is what she remembers. Truth to me is what people like Miss Jane remember."[3]

GAINES: Yes, because it's all in what you remember and in what you want to say, what's important to you. Here is this little old lady, Miss Jane. She believes in what she's saying, and she's as good as anybody else. What she says is as good and true as what anyone else says.

MG: Her perspective is equally valid.

GAINES: Yes.

MG: Do you think that the South Louisiana setting, with that sort of unique mixture of French and Cajun and black, makes your writing different from that of other southern writers? Or do you see yourself basically as a southern writer or a Louisiana writer?

GAINES: I see myself as a writer, and I happen to have been born here. I was born black. I was born on a plantation. I've lived in that interracial, or ethnic, mixture of the Cajun, and the big house owned by the Creoles—not Cajuns, but Creoles—and the blacks. I was associated very early with the Baptist church; I was christened as a Baptist. But I went to Catholic school, a little school in New Roads, my last three years in Louisiana. I had to go through their kind of discipline. I had to go to mass. I didn't go to confession or anything like that. I didn't take the Holy Sacrament. I had to go through all these kinds of things. My aunt who raised me and who was crippled spoke Creole. Some of the old ladies on the plantation and some of the old men spoke Creole. I traveled around with another aunt of mine who sold the little cosmetic things all over Pointe Coupée and West Baton Rouge parishes, and I met all these people who put these things on their faces and made themselves smell sweet, and they spoke French because my aunt spoke Creole.

I am a different writer from, say, Faulkner, and I'm a different writer from a lot of black writers. A writer from North Louisiana would not have had the same experiences I had in South Louisiana. One who came from Mississippi or Alabama or Georgia or Texas

3. Ernest J. Gaines, "Miss Jane and I," *Callaloo*, I (1978), 37.

would not have had the same experience. I never think of myself as, number one, a black writer, quote "black," or "Louisiana black," but as a writer who happens to draw from his environment what his life is, what his heritage is. I try to put that down on paper.

I think my work is unique in that, I think, I come from a place that is quite unique, certainly very different from all the rest of the southern states. Louisiana has a tremendous romantic history about it, the Spanish and the French and all those things. We're just a different group, and we have problems maybe others don't have or don't pay so much attention to. I think we have a big problem among the darker-skinned and the fairer-skinned black people in this state, more than in any other state in the Union. I see it all the time, and I live it. I saw it in New Orleans just this last week, and I've seen it in areas around Lafayette and Baton Rouge. I've experienced that. This guy was talking to me about our African ancestry, and he looks as African as I look Japanese. I'm pretty sure that, deep down inside, they don't look at themselves as being "black" as I look at myself being black.

MG: That's the kind of thing you handle in *Catherine Carmier*. It's an identity problem, because, obviously, they have not identified themselves as white either.

GAINES: Right. That's one of the things about Lillian. Lillian says: "Hey, listen, wait awhile. I cannot live in this middle-of-the-road kind of situation. I cannot cross this fence anymore. I'm white enough to go over there, and I'm going to make this choice. I'm going over there because I can't live across this fence anymore, the way I've been trained to do." And I saw a lot of people at the museum in New Orleans the other night who could have gone one way or the other. And yet they're saying they are black. But they don't feel that way—they don't feel that they are.

MG: In Louisiana it's always been something more like an ethnic identity, linked to the idea of the Creole of color. This group of fair-skinned people of black and Creole descent were at one time, if not almost a separate race, at least a separate ethnic group, who prided themselves on being neither black nor white.

GAINES: That's what all the Creole stuff is about right now, because if you think about it, there's no such thing as a Creole with mixed blood. There's no such thing as a Creole with African ancestry. But that is the one identity they could use: "I'm not black, I'm not white, I'm Creole." That is a falseness in itself, because the Creoles were either French or Spanish.

MG: Of course, right now *Creole* is usually used to mean "mixed-blood."

GAINES: Well, this is what I mean. You can easily say that: "I'm not black, but I'm Creole." And most of them hide behind this until it becomes necessary, in politics or whatever, in order to get what you need to accomplish, [to] say, "I'm black." But I think that, deep down inside, they know they haven't paid their dues. Too many black people got murdered and bled to change this thing in the South while these people hung back. Yet because they were closer in their features to the Caucasians, closer to the whites in power, they were the ones who could get in much easier than the black ones who had to die for it. They were not black when they had to go out there and die in the streets and suffer in the streets as the blacks had to do.

I think it was your [CW's] class I was in, and this kid sat in the back—a dark-skinned kid, almost as dark as I am—and he said that he never heard of anything like that in his family. I didn't want to call the kid a liar. He said that his ancestry were those people that I talked about. I cannot imagine a family made up of a mixture of darker people and fairer people who have not had these problems. I had it in my family.

MG: Your portrayals of Cajuns seldom show their positive characteristics and values as strong, hard-working, congenial, family-oriented people. What does the word *Cajun* mean to you?

GAINES: I don't know. It depends on—I think I could ask the same question, as what does *black* or *Negro* mean to you? And I think it depends on your education, your intelligence, your knowledge of people. I think I have a different interpretation of what Cajun means than what my stepfather's interpretation of Cajun was. Now, to my stepfather and people of his generation, Cajun meant a white who would give them hell on False River, because it's been known that this would happen since the time a Cajun killed this man in 1903. And anytime there was a problem on the river, and because so many of the whites there were Cajun, it would always be "that Cajun," whether one of them was involved or not. This is what the whole Fix thing in *A Gathering of Old Men* is about; it's what Mapes is talking about.

Now, that does not mean the same thing to me, because I'm quite aware of the difference. I think I've learned more about the difference since I've been here at USL, but I think I was aware of the difference between mine and my stepfather's interpretation even when I was a child growing up. I never did face what he faced as a young man growing up, probably in the early twenties or in the late teens. It's a different world.

CW: This had to do a great deal with competition for the land, didn't it?

GAINES: Well, it was competition for the land in some respects. In others it was not, because my stepfather did not work on a plantation. It was competition for the land, competition for the river. I suppose socially there was competition. My older people always felt, well, hell, we're as good as anybody else. I have a real unique family, because we never felt inferior to people. We may not have been able to speak Creole, but that didn't mean we were inferior to those who could. Really, they spoke half French and half English, and we thought if we could speak English a little better, hell, we were the superior ones. I think that by the time we got there, we did not associate any problems between white and black on False River as a Cajun problem. But I think in the time of my stepfather and his generation, it was.

Of course, you must blame somebody, and just as the whites always blamed the blacks, the Cajun was blamed as the one who did something. You know, if one black does something wrong back-of-town, here comes the redneck cop, and he's going to come in there. At a certain time—I wouldn't put it as now—but at a certain time, he would come in there, and he'd take as many as he thinks he needs to make one of them tell what happened. So he's using all blacks over here. So when something happened with a white, the blacks said "those Cajuns" just the way the whites said "those niggers back there."

CW: For your stepfather, did the word *Cajun* have connotations similar to the word *nigger* for the whites at that time?

GAINES: I don't think so. I think to them it was just a white man who spoke French. I don't think he meant it to be derogatory. My stepfather was a very strong man, a very handsome man, a very powerfully built man. And there's no way that he felt that anybody was better than he. He had property. They were property people. They had land. A different thing would be with where I come from, the plantation, after it was turned to sharecropping. Then it did become a competitive thing because my people knew darned well they got the worst part of the land. They knew their land was not as good as the land the Cajuns received from those same people my people had worked for for so many years.

MG: Until maybe fifteen or so years ago, when there developed an increased ethnic awareness and pride, the word *Cajun*, when used by other white people in the area, was certainly a derogatory term. They meant it as an insult.

GAINES: How else would they have defined that particular group?

CW: It really had to do with identifying a group that couldn't speak English well enough.

MG: They lacked education, were poorer, perhaps.

GAINES: Well, suppose that person was a professor or teacher. He would not have been considered a Cajun?

MG: He would have been of Acadian descent, of course, but not necessarily part of the Cajun culture. Now there is pride in being a Cajun.

GAINES: I see. Well, that's a different thing from what the blacks would do, because the blacks would just say "those Cajuns over there." They're the ones who spoke French.

MG: When you came back here to live in '81, what were the changes that either disturbed you the most or surprised you the most in South Louisiana?

GAINES: I'm speaking for myself, not the average black out there. I don't think the average person who's out there will come into USL and get the same treatment socially as I do. I've been around very well-educated and middle-class whites for most of my adult life, and I've been around people in English, people interested in writing and art. So when I came here, I just found I could easily fall into this same sort of thing because the people here were speaking the same language that the people spoke in San Francisco or at Stanford. There was no shock, no cultural shock, as long as I'm on campus and the different places here, in your home and your home. In those places I see no difference between here and there.

There are times when you notice a difference, when you're in other situations. But nothing traumatic has happened. Oh, I remember driving my car—all my cars break down—but I was driving out there, and that damned thing stopped on me just as I got out of Arbolado [the residential area in which Gaines lives]. It just stopped in the street in heavy traffic. And there was a little fellow who got out and started calling me every kind of nigger in the world from his pickup truck. Everybody else was sort of moving around, because I was blocking one of the lanes, but I was not blocking them all. He could have easily moved around, but he just wanted a confrontation. I guess when I started getting out of the car, he could see his size was not comparable to my size, so he just went on.

But, I mean, that sort of thing can happen. I've been in several places both here and in Baton Rouge since I've been back here, having a sherry or a cognac with people. I would not have been in there drinking sherry with them forty, fifty years ago, but I'm pretty sure they could not have talked any worse about their servants back then than they were at that particular time. These were the kinds of things I've confronted, but they were not speaking directly to me, because we were drinking sherry together. They were not talking to me. They were talking about someone else. Still, they were talking about a black.

I remember I was picking up some things for my office at one of these used furniture places, and I was asking about them, and the person said, "I think I have some stacked up back in the corner, but I don't know if you'd want them." I said, "Well, I'd like to see them anyhow." He said, "Well, OK, I'll get my boy to get them out for you." I just sort of glanced back over my shoulder and I saw a young white guy, and then there was a black guy who must've been in his forties. I just assumed he had meant the young white kid in his teens, but he was talking about the black. A middle-aged man! "I'll get my boy over there to do that sort of thing"!

I've heard it once here in Arbolado and once in Baton Rouge, and these sorts of things, well, they're there, just as the thing that happened in New Roads the other day. When I met Volker [Volker Schlondorf, the director of the film version of *A Gathering of Old Men*] to talk about the filming—this was in New Roads—we were trying to find a place just to sit and have coffee and talk about things. Volker had taken a lot of pictures all over the place—St. Francisville, Thibodaux—and we were walking along the street, Volker, the German woman he was with, and I. Volker said, "Maybe this woman over here would know." And I went up to her and said, "Pardon me, miss"—she owned a store and she was hanging things out on a rack in front of her store—"could you tell me where there's a place where we could have some coffee?" She hung a dress or something before she said anything, and then she just turned directly from me to talk to Volker and the woman, to give them directions.

Volker and the woman pretended they had not noticed anything. I wished they had not, but after we were sitting and talking he told me, "I saw what this woman did." I said, "It was nothing shocking, really." It embarrasses me that he saw it! But these kinds of things can happen. I'm pretty sure they can happen in Lafayette just as they've happened in New Roads.

6
Fiction into Film

CW: What is your response to what was done with the movie of *A Gathering of Old Men* in relation to your book?

GAINES: I think they did a pretty good job.

CW: This is the third work of yours that has been filmed?

GAINES: *A Gathering of Old Men* is the third work, yes. *The Autobiography of Miss Jane Pittman* was first, and "The Sky Is Gray" was made by the "American Short Story" series for public television. *A Gathering of Old Men* is the third.

CW: We've talked before about things you've noticed in the other films. For example, in "The Sky Is Gray," they used a cornfield instead of a canefield, big birds instead of little scrawny ones, and the sky never was gray.

GAINES: It was pale blue all the time.

CW: Does that bother you?

GAINES: No, it doesn't bother me, because by the time you make a film of a book, the writer—unless he's a one-book writer—has just about forgotten that book, and he's gone to something else. And it's a different medium altogether. You just feel like, OK, let them do what they want to do. You know, take the money and do something well with the money. Buy something, invest the money if it's enough, and if not, just pay off the bills. And you just hope that they'll make a decent film and the people will watch it and those people will go out and buy the book. It's the book that you're much more interested in selling than you are the film.

MG: You're much more interested in having people read your work.

GAINES: Of course, of course. I want people to read my book. Whether it's a good film or a bad film, people will go out and get that book. Once they've seen the name of the book and the writer several times, they will have a tendency to buy the book. *Miss Jane Pittman* is a very good example. Before the filming, I think we'd had only about three editions, three printings, in hardback, and I think about three or four printings in paperback. But since then we've had, say, twelve printings in hardback. After fifteen *years*, it was reissued in hardback. Since the film, we've had about twenty, twenty-two, twenty-three printings in paperback of *The Autobiography of Miss Jane Pittman*, and I'm pretty sure it's because it was made into a film. And because of that film, many colleges and high schools have included the book as a part of the curriculum. Because of the film, they've used that book. Even a bad film will get people interested in the book.

MG: With the first two, "The Sky Is Gray" and *Miss Jane Pittman*, were you pleased with the film versions?

GAINES: I think if you want to measure something on a scale of one to ten, let's say *Miss Jane Pittman* was maybe a five, and then "The Sky Is Gray" about the same. With *Miss Jane Pittman*, you could not get the entire story of a hundred years in two hours. You had to choose points, pieces, and then try to mold that into a whole. In "The Sky Is Gray," the main character is a little boy about eight years old, and they could not find a little boy eight years old to carry the story. So they had to get a larger boy about thirteen years old—and that makes a difference on the effect of the story. It makes a big difference.

CW: The novel about Miss Jane uses the first-person point of view. It's very difficult for the camera to do that, to look at the character and through the eyes of the character at the same time.

GAINES: Something was said about the filming of Flaubert's *Madame Bovary*. In the book you can smell the cabbage cooking. In the film you never could smell the cabbage. There are certain things that you do capture, things that you do put on the screen. There are certain things in the book that you cannot put on the screen, many things. You can put action on the screen, but I don't know that you can put thoughts and dreams and, really, the depth of the personality on the screen. I don't know that you can put that on the screen.

CW: How much of the filming of *A Gathering of Old Men* did you get to watch?

GAINES: I went down three weekends to Thibodaux, where it

was filmed. I went on Saturdays and watched the shooting. They didn't shoot on Sundays, and I stayed until Monday evening. Out of all the shooting, which took about a month, I saw about six days of it.

CW: You said that you were apart from the process of making your book into a movie. You were really just an observer.

GAINES: As I said before, since they didn't tell me how to write the book, I would not tell them how to make their film.

CW: What's your feeling about what you saw those six days you were there?

GAINES: There are lots of things you can criticize anytime someone makes something else out of your work. I'm sure Shakespeare could have criticized productions of his work. Tolstoy or Faulkner, you know. God with the Bible. [Laughter] Somebody is going to have to pay for it when they get up there with Him. They're going to have to pay for what they did. They'll line up and they'll have to pay Faulkner and Hemingway and Shakespeare for what they've done to their works.

There's a story about Brahms. He saw one of his concertos being conducted by some crazy gypsy. This guy was just bouncing and jumping in the air directing the orchestra, and Brahms just sat there. At the end, someone asked him, "Herr Brahms, what do you think?" And Brahms said, "So, it can be done like that, too." And really, this is what you do. You say: "So, well, it can be done like that. I didn't know that." I didn't know when I was writing it that it could be done that way. There are quite a few things they did that I didn't care about. They took liberties with dialogue. They changed the dialogue I had written, and they used their own dialects.

MG: What about the dialect? Often in movies made in places like Louisiana where there is a definite dialect and accent, actors tend to exaggerate to the point that it becomes almost offensive to the people.

GAINES: That's absolutely true. When actors and others don't come down here and listen to people, or when they don't read a particular novel or short story carefully, they tend to write all dialects alike. And we definitely are different in South Louisiana from people in Mississippi or Alabama or Georgia or Texas. You try to correct it if you can speak to them or if they approach you. Quite often they don't want you around. Fortunately for me, the people who made the three films that have been made from my works, *Miss Jane*, "The Sky Is Gray," and *A Gathering of Old Men*, have all asked me to come around, not to give suggestions, but to be there. And occasionally an actor or producer or the director will ask me how to use a certain term. Quite often it's going to be different from what I have written. They changed names of characters. Instead of thirteen, or whatever number of old men I have speaking in the book, there are about six or seven speaking. They combined characters, taking the dialogue from two or three characters and giving it to one. They changed the clothes. They changed the size of the characters. In *A Gathering of Old Men*, the character Mapes is big. Richard Widmark, who plays Mapes, is thin. These are changes that are done.

Fortunately, before we started shooting the film, Volker Schlondorf asked me to take him to the place where I had grown up. I showed him the house there so he could have an idea what the house looked like. I think he really re-created it. The house that they have in the film is just like the one that I showed him. The road is quite a bit like the real road. The scenery is quite authentic. It was the dialogue which they tried to change a lot when they started combining things. When they started taking a few lines from here and a few lines from there and putting them together into one speech and adding their own terms to it—that's when they took liberties I did not approve of. But as I said, I'm not part of it. I'm not in the film-making business.

MG: Do you think they maintained the humor and the comic aspects?

GAINES: That is one of the things I'm afraid does not really come through. During the time I was there watching the shooting, I didn't see too many people laughing. I'll tell you that right now. Sometimes they don't speak the lines exactly the way I wrote them. For example, Widmark is supposed to say something that is very funny, but he does not say it funny. I told Volker, "I didn't hear any laughter," and he said, "Well, you can't hear laughter here, because it was not meant for those people to laugh." And he said, "You'll hear laughter from the audience." And I said, "Ohhhh." I said, "I'm the audience now, and I didn't laugh, so I don't know whether or not I'll laugh later at the television screen." I wasn't laughing at all at that line Widmark was saying.

I was talking with a newspaper guy from Florida. He said, "How can you bring a German in here to direct a film?" I said: "I didn't bring him in. The producer is British, and he brought this German guy. This guy is a very famous director." He says: "But does he know American humor? Does he know American mood?" He says you can't just bring anybody and say, "Now make this thing funny." You can bring anybody and make it dramatic, but you can't come in and make it funny. He must know the subtleties in order to bring this off and bring the humor out of that story. It just didn't come off.

CW: Many of the things they tried to do to give it humor were things that they added that you didn't put in, like the car backing into the hearse.

GAINES: That was cheap Hollywood.

MG: They missed the subtleties.

GAINES: For example, the scene where the actor Griffin says, "Why don't we just throw the old coon in the back of the car and get out of here?" Woody spoke the line—but he wasn't supposed to—and he says, "He's got a big mouth for hardly any butt." That's supposed to be funny the way he said it. The character [Griffin] must be a very thin person, then you can laugh about the whole thing. This guy was not that thin.

CW: You laugh about the line, but you look at Griffin and it's not funny anymore.

GAINES: Things like that. And when he says that, the next line is supposed to be, "Pardon me, ladies," because he's supposed to be thinking he can't use a word like that in front of a lady. Then Mapes is supposed to say: "Oh, forget it. We're all one big happy family. You don't have to say 'pardon me' to the white lady anymore." This whole thing is supposed to come off, but it didn't. It shot by you, and they're not preparing for the pause of humor. Things like this don't come off, because I don't think Volker knows how to make the pause.

CW: The humor depends on an idiomatic sense of the language.

GAINES: There you are. And humor depends on that sense of

pausing. That's why Jack Benny was one of the greatest humorists. Jack Benny knew how to give pause. He could see a line and, just like that, give the right pause to the line.

A very simple thing, too—I don't dislike producers, but producers are always getting on directors to rush things, rush things. Volker would tell me: "Ernie, I can't rest. They're rushing me and all I can do is work. I'm out on that set twelve hours, and they're rushing me, and I'm thinking about the damned thing another four or five hours." I know they did the same thing to the director of *The Autobiography of Miss Jane Pittman*, just working him to death, instead of taking just one more week and letting these guys do their stuff.

One of these days, a scholar is going to get the book and run that film piece by piece, and they're going to find all the mistakes. There are so many mistakes of lines, so many mistakes of changing around names. For example, the guy who shoots at the rabbit is Uncle Billy, and then when they come into the cemetery and Clatoo says, "Did everybody shoot?" Here's Woody again, [they're] giving Woody the line, and Woody says, "Yeah, Chimley shot at a rabbit on his foot and missed." All these mistakes are because they're rushing, rushing, and they don't have time to concentrate well enough on what is going on without changing the names. There's so much pressure to go on; if a line doesn't come off, they don't repeat it.

MG: Why don't directors pay more attention to the expertise of the author and the local people?

GAINES: Sometimes he doesn't have time. But it's not only the director. It can be the scriptwriter. For example, Schlondorf doesn't know a damned thing about the South. He directed *Death of a Salesman*, but that's an internationally known play. He doesn't know the nuances of the South. He doesn't know the people, the Cajuns, the blacks, the great landowners. He doesn't know the architecture of the houses. I know damned well he doesn't know southern Louisiana. Where I think he came through very well was when he went into Fix's house. I think he was powerful as hell. But then he was dealing with something that would be common to Europe, the situation, the people gathering, the eating—

CW: The autocratic father who rules his house—

MG: He does a much better job with the drama.

GAINES: Once he gets in there with the situation that can be explosive, say in Tee Jack's place—they changed that around so pathetically, till it was so bad—it comes off, if you don't know the book. But when he has to come out and spend those long hours with those people just sort of hanging around, waiting, there's no tension in the waiting there. There's no suspense in the waiting. There can be much suspense in waiting for something, just waiting. We had the characters out there who could bring that off. We had Julius Harris, the one in the army uniform. And we had Woody Strode. Woody can wait! I've seen Woody in one of these old Italian films, *Once Upon a Time in the West*, just waiting for this train to come in because he was going to kill a guy who was coming in on the train. And just moving a face toward the railroad track, that's what tension is. And I know damned well Joe Seneca, who plays Clatoo, can bring off anything—that's one of the great actors.

But you don't have that! You don't have this tension. You have people moving around, throwing a baseball around the place, but the tension is not there. Every moment is supposed to be waiting for Fix, and that's why when Widmark/Mapes says Fix isn't showing up, that's a lie to the old men, and they're still waiting. There's concentration on the waiting: "That's a lie. He's got to show up. We know he's coming in. We know!" And yet he's not. He does it thirty years ago. They've been waiting so hungrily, and you don't find that [in the film].

CW: The first thing that struck me as a mistake was after Candy talked to Snookum. He went off to deliver her message, but he added information that she never told him.

GAINES: What had happened was, another guy had played the part. Snookum just had to run to the house. That's all he had to do in the beginning. They had another guy, a great big old guy the way I have him in the book, and the scene didn't come off well enough, and the guy had gone. Volker said he didn't like that scene, but the producer wasn't going to bring the actor back because he didn't want to pay the money. So he got Snookum to play the scene, which was awful. Now, Snookum could have played it in the beginning if Candy had told him. These are the kinds of things that you find when people are under such pressure to get something done.

CW: And it's pure economics.

GAINES: Definitely so. And some of the scenes—for example, where those old men are fishing: that's an awful scene, where those boats are in the water. I never described anything like that. If you look at False River, it's one of the most beautiful lakes there is. The river is not destroyed. The places are built up. You don't have this trash there. I think what happened was that where they were shooting this film, on that plantation, there were two or three old abandoned cars, and that must have struck Volker as [being] what Americans do: they just dump things on the side because they have so much.

So they come to the river scene, and the old man says, "These white folks know how to destroy a place." I never said that! I said there are places you can't go to fish anymore because the place is so built up now. All these condos, these townhouses, are built on the water, and forty years ago, these things were not there. You could just walk down the road and fish and go home anytime you wanted to.

CW: What about the scene with the little old lady at the end?

GAINES: I have no comment on that damned thing. I have no idea what they were doing. I don't know why she's sitting there. I don't know a damned thing about that scene. When I saw it in the script—I didn't see them actually shoot the scene—I asked Volker: "What the hell is that last thing? What's this with Corinne sitting there?" And he said, "I think it's a good scene." And I said, "Well, is she dead?"

MG: People couldn't quite figure out whether or not she was dead.

GAINES: Right. And I know Candy touched her and there's no response and she drew her hand back.

CW: But Candy didn't show much emotion either.

GAINES: And you don't know whether she's alive or dead. So I still don't know what the hell she's supposed to be doing.

MG: Carl thought maybe they had read "Just Like a Tree" and decided to put in another ending.

GAINES: Maybe Charles Fuller [the scriptwriter] did. I'm pretty sure Charles Fuller has read it. Now, it's the first time the old men have stood up to something, and the old lady has seen this, and she can die happily. That's as good an answer to it as anything I can come up with.

MG: The scene goes by too quickly. Earlier you said that the director said the actor didn't need bulk to portray Mapes. Do you think that came across?

GAINES: It would not have come across if they had had the ending that I had. But since they changed the ending around, I guess it could. I think the guy who plays the coroner is damned good. He gets out, and he's wiping his brow, and he has to lean on something to bend over that body. He's panting, and he speaks his lines well, except for the very first line. "What the hell is going on around here, Mapes?" It should be spoken, "What the HELL is going on around here?" Economics again. You can't go over it again. You keep moving.

Some of the scenes that they did—for example, the slapping scenes—they did over and over and over. The scene where they lined up to be beaten, they went over that thing I bet a dozen times. He really hit Uncle Billy—Sandman Sims—and they're friends, Widmark and Sims. With friends like that, I wouldn't want any enemies. He knocked the hell out of him. He was supposed to just knock that hat off, but he came a little lower and knocked the hell out of him.

MG: One thing that everyone seemed pleased with was that Lou Gossett, Jr., plays Mathu. How did you feel about it when you saw it being filmed?

GAINES: I saw Gossett in a couple of scenes, which were fantastic. One was the scene before Charlie returns, and the old men gather in Mathu's house, and he's telling them that they should go home. He's going to take responsibility. Gossett really speaks that scene very, very well.

When I was told that he was in the film, I couldn't really imagine his being Mathu because Gossett is, I think, fifty, and what you could say good-looking. But then Cicely [Tyson] was much younger when she played Miss Jane. Cicely was still in her thirties when she played someone who was 110. As soon as I saw Gossett in the makeup, I knew he could do it because he had all the mannerisms of someone seventy years old. When Gower Frost, the producer, told me that Richard Widmark was playing Mapes, I thought, "Good Lord!" But then when you see it done, you can see that these guys are very good at it.

We were discussing characters one day before they started shooting. Gower Frost and I were talking about Charlie, and I was trying to show him how important it was that Charlie be big, so that when Charlie comes back, this huge guy comes back and people look up to him. And Volker—Volker's very short—said, "People can look at a short man the same way." And I said: "Well, I like bulk. Charlie should be bulk." And they did get someone like that, Walter Breaux. He is big. I have a picture of me standing between Walter and the guy playing Beau [Boutan, the murder victim]. These guys both weigh over 300 pounds. I weigh 225, and I look small. These are huge men.

MG: What about the actress who plays Candy?

GAINES: I think most of her work has been done in New York. Her name is Holly Hunter. Will Patton, who was in *Belizaire the Cajun*, plays Lou Dimes. Woody Strode plays Yank, along with about three other characters. I think Dirty Red's lines are thrown in. A few other characters' dialogue is thrown in.

CW: They didn't seem to reduce the number of old men who gather.

GAINES: No. They have all the old men there. They just don't have them all speaking.

MG: Uncle Billy speaks, but they didn't include his comic scene with the sheriff.

GAINES: No, no, no. That was cut out. It was a comic thing, very, very funny, but they cut it out. In the novel, Mapes sends his deputy, Griffin, to pick out one of the old men to bring up to where Mapes is. Instead of doing that, Widmark, playing Mapes, calls the guys to him. It's changed around to speed it up a little bit. Widmark says, "Uncle Billy, come down here." So Billy comes over to him, and Widmark asks him, "OK, what's going on?" And the guy says, "I shot him."

Someone mentioned that Widmark's most famous film is *Kiss of Death*. He was very young then. In that film he's looking for Victor Mature, who is supposed to have ratted on the gang. Widmark goes to Victor Mature's house and finds the old mother in a wheelchair. Widmark asks, "Where's the rat?" and she says, "I don't know. I don't know." So Widmark pulls the telephone cord out of the wall, ties her up and, pushes her down the stairs and kills her. Someone commented that Widmark started his reputation by pushing old white women downstairs, and now he's ending his reputation by slapping old black men around.

CW: The most obvious change was at the ending. Did they give reasons for doing it the way they did it?

GAINES: No, no, they gave me no reason at all. When they came down here to shoot the film, they told me they had changed the ending. He said, "I think it's for the best, and I think you'll like it."

CW: Did you?

GAINES: I don't know that I like it or not. It's OK with me. I never argue with what they do in Hollywood. They have their own way of communicating with an audience, and I don't argue with it. When I think about it on *The Autobiography of Miss Jane Pittman*, most people remember the film by the ending of it, the walk to the fountain, which I did not write. So I feel these people can do what they want to do, and there's nothing you can do about it. I don't know that my ending was the best ending. The way I had it down, I thought I was trying to prove a point.

CW: What do you see as the difference between the points that were made by the different endings?

GAINES: I don't know if there's any difference at all. I think what I was trying to do in that entire book was show a group of old men standing. They brought guns, and I still believe in the old Chekhovian idea that if the gun is over the mantel at the beginning of the play, the gun must go off by the time the curtain comes down. And I thought that the only way the gun could go off in my book was Charlie and Luke Will out on the street shooting at each other. They felt they didn't have to stick too close to Chekhov.

MG: You wonder how much [of] it would be just the difficulty of filming that scene, and whether they could've brought it across with the comic aspects you put into it.

GAINES: I think they could have captured it. I think they could have brought that off if they had wanted to do that. I think if this film had been made for theater, they could have done that, and they maybe would have. But this is done for television, and maybe they just didn't want a black and white shootout, killing each other off. This would be my guess. I have no idea why they did it. They don't explain any-thing to me.

MG: One of the reactions that we've gotten is that people felt disappointed, that they wanted to see that ending.

GAINES: I know. I heard from New York, when it was shown to the press, that there were people who were disappointed with the ending. They wanted to see the ending as I had written it.

MG: Those comments may lead even more people to read the book.

GAINES: I hope that people who don't like these kinds of things would do something about it by writing to CBS or to TV Guide and saying, "We thought the way the book did it was so much better." Not that it's going to change anything, but maybe some of the letters would be printed, and that could cause some minor controversy, and more people read the book.

MG: The comments in general have been that [viewers were] disappointed with the way they changed the ending.

GAINES: Well, yes. I was talking to someone today, and he was saying the same thing. He said that he did not feel that Mapes really came off as mean and brutal as he was in the book. They were playing down certain characters. They played Mapes's character down, and they did not see the gradual change in Mapes. They do that, and they take more liberties when you're dealing with television, because they try to make it palatable for television. A lot of people just don't want to see people shooting each other.

CW: They're also working within a more rigid time frame. A theater movie can run five or six minutes extra or whatever it takes.

MG: One of the other comments that I've heard is that, after having Lou Gossett to play that role, they made the role so small. Did you feel as though they had really minimized Mathu's role as com-pared to the book, in which he is so obviously central?

GAINES: I think so. One of the reasons that happened was that [Volker] really wanted to enlarge Woody Strode's part. In each scene, if you can recall, Strode was getting more and more lines to say than anyone else because Volker kept Woody up front all the time. And he combined him into two different characters, which he should not have done. He combined Dirty Red and Yank, and that's just like trying to mix oil and water. Dirty Red is slouchy, and he drags the gun along. Yank is a very proud person. He'd never drag his gun the way you see Woody is doing in his opening scene. And that funny-looking little cap—Yank is supposed to wear a cowboy hat. So you have this trying to give him so many parts to play at one time, building him up in every scene, and minimizing Mathu's role played by Lou Gossett. I never did know he had so few speaking parts. My main criticism is that you see him there all the time, but at the very end, he is supposed to have a long speech in that house when they're together in there, and this is minimized.

CW: When you were watching the filming, was there much more to it that just ended up being edited out?

GAINES: There was more written into the script than that. I saw the script. Then they cut it out. They felt there was something that might be anti-Christian or antireligious, but that was part of his character. All he was trying to say was: "Listen, you guys have made me very happy today, and I'm changed, I'm converted. I'm just like a converted person who's found religion, but it was not that white man's God. He didn't have nothing to do with any of this. You were the ones who did this." Then he goes down the line, and he says this guy did this, and this guy, and he goes to about three or four different guys and says, look, these people here are the ones that made these changes in this man's life. "I've been bitter all my life. I've hated you because you wouldn't try. I hated those out there because they denied me." And he explained to them why, and he said OK, I'll fall back on my Africanism, proud to be African. So all he said in the film was about two lines, where it should have been about two paragraphs, about two minutes of talking, and they give him about fifteen, thirty seconds.

MG: Do you think Will Patton created the kind of person you had in mind for Lou Dimes?

GAINES: Will wasn't the kind of guy I had in mind. The guy was supposed to be tall, a basketball player.

CW: I agree with Marcia about the diminishing of the role of Mathu, but at the same time, one effect of that was to make sort of a collective star out of all the old men.

GAINES: The concentration was on Woody Strode more than any of the other men, and on Joe Seneca, too. At the scene where Seneca calls on his brother Silas—"I just stood there and let them beat up my brother, because I was paralyzed by fear"—another actor was supposed to speak those lines. However, Volker—and I thought he made a good move there—said he thought Joe Seneca could bring that off better than anyone else, because he wanted some closeups on this guy's face. And I agree with him on that.

I didn't particularly agree with the opening scenes, where Charlie is running, because the thing is a mystery. For example, we don't know who killed Beau. I still don't know who killed Beau, and I wrote the damned thing three or four years ago. Mathu could have very easily killed Beau. As a matter of fact, the first draft, I wrote with Mathu being the killer. In the opening scene of the film, you have to grasp the attention of the audience. Everything is getting the audience's attention because if you don't, they're going to turn that television off. So you're coming down there with this guy with a shotgun chasing another guy, and that's Hollywood stuff.

Of course, you know the book, and I didn't write it that way. He doesn't know if this actually happened that way. You're supposed to think back on it, and Charlie tells, at the very end, what happens to him. You could easily rewrite that entire opening scene. When Gil comes on the scene, he says: "Beau never would have chased Charlie with a gun. Beau would have come in this yard with a piece of sugarcane and beat Charlie, but not to shoot him." That's what Gil says. Let's say it happened that way, and when Mathu sees that Charlie's going to run, Mathu warns Beau—let's just rewrite this scene— Mathu warns Beau: "Don't you come in my yard. Don't you cross that ditch. Sugarcane or no sugarcane, don't cross my ditch." And when Beau comes in there, Mathu kills him. You'd have a mystery there. But the way it is in the film, you don't have a mystery. The mystery is a Hollywood-created mystery.

CW: It's a mystery with an easy solution.

GAINES: That's the Hollywood thing, the easiest way to do it. That's the Hollywood way to do it. And I can understand why they must grasp the attention of the audience. I tell my students, "Don't use cheapness to grasp attention, but your opening scenes must get the reader's attention." But you can get the reader's attention by good writing just as much, just putting the words down. Someone once said poetry is two words meeting for the first time. So what you do with writing is write well and get the effect that no one has ever read this before. But that's another story, and that's why I don't like to get into these things. You cannot tell these people how to make a film. These people know how to get your attention.

Here's this guy coming down there on a tractor with a gun, and he's saying, "I'm going to kill you, I'm going to kill you, boy!" And then, after the tractor stops, you see him loading the gun. That's pretty stupid, to see him coming along with an empty shotgun, unless he just wants to frighten him. Another thing, if they're going to start it like this, why not see the fight?

CW: Let Charlie pick up a piece of cane and hit Beau.

GAINES: Doggone right. Doggone right. In the story Charlie says, "Beau hit me twice before I struck back." In the film he says, "I'm forty years old." In the book he says, "I'm fifty years old, I'm half a hundred years old, and you shouldn't talk to me that way." And Beau says, "I'll not only talk to you that way, I'll beat the hell out of you," and Charlie says, "No, I can't let you do that to me anymore." And Beau comes after him, and then Charlie picks up a piece of cane and strikes back. We could have had that whole thing.

MG: That cane tractor was more exotic than anything else.

GAINES: That's why they got Richard Whaley to play the part: because nobody else on the set could drive a tractor.

CW: Something that others have commented on was when Miss Merle brings the sandwiches and they leave out all her saying "Lord, Jesus!" over and over. That's a kind of humor they lost.

GAINES: There you are. They put that little stupid dog out there, but that didn't make up for the lines. Those lines are the thing. I know how to write dialogue. By damn it, that's the strongest point in my work. I know how to write dialogue, and I know how a southern woman with all this energy like Miss Merle—I know how she'd speak.

CW: That leads to another question. With that sense of wanting to get it right, would you consider helping with the film?

GAINES: If they'd asked me, I would have sat down with

Charles Fuller and said, OK, what do we do? Let Charles Fuller draw up the entire thing—scene here, scene here, scene here—and then say, would you like to write the extra dialogue? Damned right I'd like to do it. And I would do it for nothing. All of this deal about passing out these sandwiches, that was supposed to be funny.

CW: And the other one we were disappointed with was the "You can't see what we don't see" scene.

GAINES: Right, because they didn't deal with the "see." And every time Widmark says "see," the guys are supposed to get a little more angry. What he's trying to do is say, "You see weeds, you see a bunch of shacks, but you don't see these guys working, you don't see these people going to the fields, you don't see the people singing in the church. You don't see all these things that are going on through these old quarters." That was not in the screenplay itself, and yet Woody [Strode] was trying to bring it off. They were trying to bring it off with "You don't see" and the camera getting what you don't see anymore, but without the lines. The lines had to be there. It's like saying, "To be or not to be." Would you just say, "To be?" And if you don't say "or not to be," the face is supposed to bring off the rest of that line. No, bullshit, Shakespeare wrote that thing "To be or not to be," and you don't slur off those lines. Those lines are there for a reason.

They want the camera to do the work, and the camera does some great work. Good Lord, there's no one in the world who could've described that opening scene with him running down that road better than that camera did, or that opening scene with that haze in the background. But there are certain damned things that camera can't do, and that camera cannot speak lines. That camera can give a feeling of things, but that camera does not speak the lines. That camera cannot repeat rhythm. You have to use the words. You have to use everything. I mean, much of this thing is written for lines. This is not just a narrative thing, but it's a spoken thing. One time when they used the rhythm was with Jack Marshall at the very end. He says, "I don't want them niggers, I never had any niggers, I never will have any niggers." They used that well, and that was good, but I thought to myself, why the hell [use] the rhythm at this particular scene with this particular character? Why not use it where it would have been much more effective?

MG: I thought Candy seemed awfully young.

GAINES: She's about the age Candy would be. Holly Hunter's about twenty-seven. She just looks young. One thing that could've made her look younger was those tight jeans.

MG: What about Luke Will?

GAINES: Luke is a local redneck. Luke is not a Cajun. Gil says he's not a part of them. He's one of those oil drillers. He's just a local redneck who wants to keep the races apart and get into all kind of trouble he can find. And Beau would just hang around these guys, after work, having a beer over at Tee Jack's place. All this thing about Beau supposing to be this mean and brutal person—half of these old men don't even *know* Beau. The whole goddamned thing I tried to emphasize—I've said it a million times—is these old men are living in the past. They're thinking about Fix. They don't know a damned thing about Beau. He'd be so much younger than these men. By the time Beau comes along, these men have already been pushed off the land. These men don't come in contact with Beau. Beau is not these men's enemy. They remember Fix. And the whole damned thing is about remembering the past; they're living in the past. You're a southerner, I'm a southerner myself, and we all live in the goddamned past. We just can't get rid of it. We think of it all the time, and it haunts the living hell out of us. And all of a sudden, reality and the modern world catch up and break us. Look what happened to Lafayette. Oil comes in here and ruins the place. Taco Bell over here, all that kind of stuff.

CW: Just to give you an idea of different responses, I heard someone say, "Somebody in that movie was playing a great bass."

GAINES: Damned right that was good music. He's right, there's some good bass in that film. I didn't particularly care for Papa John Creach in there. How the hell that violin got off that bayou to Mathu's house, I don't know. I asked Volker how the hell that damned fiddle got there, when this man only had a gun in his hands. No explanation. I said, come on, some scholar's going to go into this thing and ask why they did this.

MG: One of the things I've wondered about is in those beautiful scenes, especially at the end, with the fires burning. But I don't think they ever burned those fields at night, not that close to the cabins.

GAINES: I don't know.

MG: That bothered me. And in his interview, Richard Widmark said that they burned the cane before they cut it. It may be a minor point, but in Louisiana the field is burned *after* the cane is cut. And Lou Gossett, I think it was, said it smelled like apple pie when they were burning it.

GAINES: When you get people together doing something—they're good actors and good directors—but when you get them together and put them in a play where they don't know a damned thing about what they're doing, you see all the errors. We're going to have to start keeping our directors, our talent, our technicians, our people here. When those people come from Hollywood or New York, say, "OK, bring Robert Redford or Paul Newman if you want to, but damn it, we know something about locale, we know how to burn off sugarcane, we know how to cut the sugarcane, we know how to tell this person how to pronounce 'Atchafalaya,' we know how to do all this ourselves, and you're going to pay us to get this thing done. These are the only conditions under which you're going to make this film." We have to be ready when they come in here.

CW: The lines that were written for Beau to speak were not Cajun. They were southern redneck.

GAINES: Because he's in the South, they're all supposed to sound alike. He's using what is supposed to be a southern way—Mississippi, Alabama, Georgia—that southerners talk to somebody else. It's not true, because he's not concentrating on the area. Whenever I'm all over the country, I say we have a very unique way of expressing ourselves in southern Louisiana. I've said this at Brown and Yale, at Stanford and Cal [University of California at Berkeley], all over the place. It's not that everyone speaks the same way. This is Cajun country, but there are other people in this place. What would be a fantastic thing would be to get Gower and Volker and Charles Fuller and myself together and have a seminar about these things.

7

Agents and Editors

MG: We've talked about the importance to you of the integrity of the writer. You've maintained that you wrote what you wanted to write about and that you wouldn't change your writing just to appeal to an audience or to sell your books. But you've also talked about the time, when you were working on one of the several drafts of *A Gathering of Old Men*, that your editor commented that you had all these people leaving from the same kind of place, and made a suggestion that you might want to change that, and you agreed. You did make the change. How do you see the relationship between writer and editor, and what kind of relationships have you had with your editors?

GAINES: The most important relationship has been not with an editor but with my agent, Dorothea Oppenheimer. [Dorothea Oppenheimer died on May 5, 1987.] She would suggest things, and it was her opinion I appreciated more than anyone else's. I dealt primarily with her. Yet, at the same time, as you mentioned, in this particular case the editor did make these suggestions. He was right. I could understand how right he was. It was a matter of expediency. What I was trying to do originally was show how all these people lived before that moment, what they did with their lives before that moment that brought them all together. I had the guy sitting on his porch, or I had the guy sitting at the river fishing, or I had the guy doing something else before he arrives at Mathu's house. And what the editor said was, have him coming to Mathu's house and have him thinking back, or have him speaking with one of the other characters in the scene, and then he can, in turn, tell that character what he was doing. That's what editors learn from television. That's what editors learn from movies. You always see the car arriving, especially on television. You don't know where he's coming from, but suddenly he arrives at a certain place like this. And through dialogue they explain where he had come from. These are the kinds of things that editors can do.

Now, when writing *The Autobiography of Miss Jane Pittman*, my editor, who was Bill Decker at Dial, told me from the beginning that the story should be told from the autobiographical point of view, and I couldn't understand what the hell he was talking about. He said let Miss Jane tell the story. I was telling it from several characters, just as I do in *A Gathering of Old Men*. The original title was "A Short Biography of Miss Jane Pittman." Well, once it was "Sketches of a Plantation," then it was "A Short Biography of Miss Jane Pittman," when everyone else tells the story after she's dead. He said that isn't working, but I couldn't understand what the hell he was talking about for a year. And then I realized, "Damn, it isn't working. It isn't going to work."

That's what a good editor can do—a good agent, too, who reads carefully. Dorothea has suggested things, more than any editor has ever done. She was an editor before she became an agent. They can make damned good suggestions. Not always. Lots of times they make suggestions that you cannot accept. I remember that Bob Gottlieb made suggestions about *In My Father's House* that I could not accept at all. So I just said, "Well, no, I disagree with you." Bill made some good suggestions for *The Autobiography of Miss Jane Pittman*, just as Doctorow made excellent suggestions for *Of Love and Dust*. Ed Doctorow was my editor-in-chief at Dial at that particular time, before he became a very famous writer. For example, when he first saw *Of Love and Dust*, he said he really liked the first part of that novel, and he really liked the last part of that novel, but the first part of that novel and the last part of that novel had nothing to do with each other. And he said I had to do one or the other with this novel, which I did. I sent it back to him in about three months, and he said it was a hundred percent improved, and he said he wanted me to run it through the typewriter just one more time. Do whatever I want, but just run it through one more time. I did, and he published it.

MG: In an article in the *Southern Review*, Jerry Bryant refers to a version in which Marcus and Louise escape.[1] How did he know that?

GAINES: Jerry and I are close friends. We used to see each other

1. Jerry H. Bryant, "Ernest J. Gaines: Change, Growth, and History," *Southern Review*, n.s., X (1974), 855.

all the time, just as I see you. And during the time I was writing the book, I'd read parts of it. I was always reading these things over at my house or his house, or part of it in a class, or something like that.

MG: So originally they did escape?

GAINES: They escaped, but it was not working out. See, the first part was tragic. That's what Ed Doctorow was saying, that the first part was tragic, but the second part was humorous. Marcus was saying: "I'm getting out of this goddamned place. I'm going to show you guys how to do it." So he started bribing people; he started getting wine or whiskey or whatever at the grocery store. He knew they weren't going to kill him, so he went and got things on credit at the grocery store, and he started selling it to the people in the quarters. They'd just take the bottle and turn it up, you know, for twenty-five cents or fifty cents, so he's accumulating money all the time. He was something like my man, you know, Snopes, in "Spotted Horses." He was something like that. He was playing all kinds of tricks on people. He'd do anything because he knew that the guy would not kill him, because he's supposed to work his way out of there. So he could do anything he wanted to do.

After doing all these things, after pulling all kinds of deals on all kinds of people, he escapes. And Doctorow says, no, Ernie, no, no, no. We don't have any poetic justice here. This guy's a killer. That guy's going to kill her [Louise] one day, and something has to work out here. If you want to make it a comic novel, make it a comic novel. He said I made it a comic thing at the end. He said that the first part was tragic and the second part was comic. He didn't say he shouldn't escape with her. He said it does not follow from the first part of the book to the latter part of the book; that the first part of the book is tragic, and you expect doom, you expect something to happen, something very terrible to happen, and then in the second part of the book he becomes a comic character and I'm having all kinds of fun with him. I told Doctorow, why the hell should he pay for it? The hell with it. Let the man get away. He was talking about balance. He was talking about form.

I didn't change it because of the social issue. I would never have changed it because of that. And that's one of the things I was saying a few minutes ago. They showed me technique and how to do things, but don't ever tell me what to write. I did not change it because, in the forties, the black was not supposed to get away, or anything like that.

CW: You mentioned that you and Jerry Bryant and others often read your stuff back and forth to each other. Do you still do that?

GAINES: No, I don't. During that time, I was working on *Of Love and Dust*, and maybe I was not too sure of what was going on. Not that I'm absolutely sure of myself now, but maybe I was not very sure of what was going on at that time. I would read it for feedback from someone like Jerry, whom I knew very well, and other friends, but since the *Of Love and Dust* thing, I've been invited so much—see, when I was reading *Of Love and Dust* to Jerry would be around '66 and early '67; we're talking about twenty years ago. Now I'm always going around different places—different colleges, universities, high schools—so I get a chance to read the stories or the manuscript, whatever I'm working on at the time, and I get feedback there, whereas before, I was not getting much feedback. So I would read at that time to friends around, to get some kind of response. I'd read something I thought was pretty good and just listen to what they were saying. Not that I would change anything because of their criticism. The only persons whose criticism I really followed—I shouldn't say "respected," but whom I felt knew enough to criticize my work—would be my agent and my editor at that time. But I would read it to different friends, especially to people who were not writers, but just friends to see how they responded to it.

MG: How did Dorothea Oppenheimer get to be your agent? Just how did you start to work with her?

GAINES: I enrolled in San Francisco State in 1955 when I came out of the army, and she had just come to the West Coast at that time. I think in either '55 or '54, she had just begun to start her agency on the West Coast. She had worked with another agency in New York, and she was starting out as an independent agent on the West Coast, in San Francisco.

At the same time, a lot of things were going on. That was the time of the whole beatnik thing. That's when everybody was in the San Francisco area—Kerouac, Ferlinghetti, Rexroth—and everybody who was writing at that time seemed like they had something to do with

San Francisco and Stanford. Stanford had a great writing program at that time, and so did Cal. Stanford is only thirty-three miles south of San Francisco. Cal is only about fifteen miles northeast of San Francisco.

So all of this energy is going on, and Dorothea came to the West Coast at that time. At the same time, the instructors on campus at State were organizing the little literary magazine called *Transfer* in '55, and its first publication would be in '56. During this time I was supposed to be writing essays. I was supposed to be in something called Expository Writing 101, but I couldn't write the essays. So I told my instructor I really couldn't do this stuff, because I was getting D's—I really was getting D's writing essays. So I said, I've been trying to write fiction. I had been trying to write fiction when I was in the army, six months earlier, over on Guam, and I had won a little contest—I think I won second—on Guam. And I said I'd like to express my ideas in the fiction form. He said, well, this is not a fiction class, but if you think you can do better than what you're doing in the composition form, go on into it.

So I wrote a short story titled "The Turtles." I have it here, a copy around the place. It was published in the very first edition of *Transfer*, which we were organizing on campus at that time. It was published in the very first edition and on page three, which was the first page of print. Dorothea, who happened to be starting her program at that time, saw it and liked the story. She made contact with my instructors at San Francisco State, and she said, "I would like to know more about Mr. Gaines." And then when we did meet, she said, "I think you have a great talent, and I would like to see your work from now on." And that was '56, and from then on she saw everything I wrote. That's how we got started. She was my agent for thirty-one years.

MG: Do you think that if she hadn't seen that story, you might've gotten a later start publishing? Did this give you confidence to go on?

GAINES: I would think so. What my instructors were doing was, they were just trying to help me to write, but they did not know the publishing houses and places to send the story to after you got it out of the class. They didn't know what to do with it. They said, well, just send it out. You know, you don't have time to do that when you're carrying fifteen or eighteen units. You don't have time to send stories out or do anything like that. So here's someone who says: "OK, you don't have to pay me a dime. I'm just beginning here, and you're beginning, and I'm interested in your work. Whenever you write something, a story, just send it on to my place, or drop it by my house, my apartment." So I know definitely it was that. And her encouragement, you know. It was not only that my instructors were encouraging me, but here's a literary agent encouraging someone. And no young writer just beginning gets that kind of attention from someone outside his immediate circle.

I'm pretty sure that sort of encouragement encouraged me to go on writing, encouraged me just to write more and send it on to her. She kept sending it out. Not that it was published. We didn't get anything published for about—well, it helped me to get into Stanford, those stories that I was writing at State at that time—but nothing was published, nationally published, for another seven years or so, although I was writing all that time.

MG: I think that's important for young writers to know that it's not a quick process.

GAINES: No way is it. No way is it.

CW: It's the thing that you and I have talked about probably more than any other one thing—that is, paying your dues. And you have no idea how long that's going to take—

GAINES: No idea.

CW: —or how much you're going to have to pay. You just have to keep paying them until it happens.

GAINES: Until it happens, if it ever happens.

CW: There's no guarantee it will.

GAINES: Right, because I know guys who were writing at the time at San Francisco State and at Stanford, and they gave it up. They had to give it up because of family and other things. One of the things I avoided and some of the things I regret today—that I don't have these kinds of family relationships. But I felt I would have to do one thing or the other. But when I got out of State—I got out of San Francisco State in 1957—I decided then I was going to give myself ten years. I had to prove within ten years, by '67, whether I could feel I was doing anything or not with the writing. So, really, exactly ten years later, with the publication of *Of Love and Dust*, was the time I began to get money out of writing. Then I began to get grants and things like that. Although I had gotten a fellowship at Stanford, it was not until later that the National Endowment for the Arts or the Rockefeller grants-in-aid, whoever, would give me money, and I could stay at home and do my work. But it was ten years, and I had given myself ten years from the time I graduated from State to really prove things to myself. Just because my agent liked what I was doing and my instructors at State liked what I was doing didn't mean that I was a writer. Because you're a good student, a bright student who has potential, doesn't mean that you're going to write anything to support yourself, ever.

CW: Which was the first book that really got you some notice?

GAINES: *Of Love and Dust* was the second book, and that got, really, some notice. And the third book was the *Bloodline* stories. I had written the *Bloodline* stories before *Of Love and Dust*, but no one would accept [them] because *Catherine Carmier*, my very first novel, got no notice at all. Nobody paid any attention to it. So when I tried to publish the stories, no one wanted them, by an unknown writer. At that time, you had to produce the novel first, and then they would get a collection of stories. So the Dial Press said, OK, you give us a novel and we'll publish two books, your novel as well as the stories. I always felt that the *Bloodline* stories were going to make my name. But I had to get another novel out, since *Catherine Carmier* had not made any kind of dent, any kind of reputation.

CW: I think in lots of ways there are some things that you do in the *Bloodline* stories that you don't do better anywhere else.

MG: They had all been published somewhere else, hadn't they?

GAINES: Oh, no, no, no, no. Only two of them had been published, "The Sky Is Gray," "Just Like a Tree," and, I think, "A Long Day in November," a shorter version. "The Sky Is Gray" came out in *Negro Digest*, "Just Like a Tree" came out in the *Sewanee Review*, and a shorter version of "A Long Day in November" came out in *Texas Quarterly*. Then I wrote "Three Men" and the title story later. But still nobody wanted to publish it. I had to produce another novel.

MG: We looked at the dedications of all your books and thought we'd ask you about them.

GAINES: All right. The first one was *Catherine Carmier*, and I said, "For S." I used to call Dorothea "Stinker." I don't want to get into any kind of discussion of it, but I remember once I forgot her birthday. She reminded me, and I went out and bought her a stuffed skunk, one of those little dolls, with a little tag around the doll's neck saying the name "Stinker." And I gave her that to remember that I did not remember her birthday. Up until she died, if she didn't call me "E.," she'd always call me "Stinker," and that was probably twenty-five years that went on like this. I called her "Stinker," and "S." was "Stinker," although I've known a couple of women whose names begin with *S*, and they swore I was writing it to them.

Of Love and Dust is for two friends of mine. As a matter of fact, they're an interracial couple, Lavelle and Alice. In fact, I had to go to Ohio when I was writing that book, and I didn't have any money. Lavelle just put five hundred bucks in my hand, and I said, "Thanks, old man, my book will be dedicated to you." I was just working on it. I didn't know if the damned thing would be published, and he didn't know. When I came back from my trip, I gave him back his money. But as I was writing about an interracial love affair in the story, and he was black and Alice was white, I just dedicated it to them.

Bloodline is to "Dee," who is Dorothea again. *Miss Jane* is to my grandmother, my aunt, and my stepfather. *A Long Day in November* is to all little boys who have had one long day in their lives. *In My Father's House*, I think I have "Mamie, George, and Octavia." Octavia is the lady whom I used to go around the parish with to sell that perfume stuff. She loved me just as she would have loved her own sons.

MG: What about George and Mamie?

GAINES: When I stayed here in '63, I stayed at their home. George is my grandmother's younger brother, but there was a different father. My grandmother was a McVey. George was a Williams. And Mamie was his wife. Mamie died on her way to California in '65. I think there were six of them trying to get to California in a car. Mamie was short and very heavy. And they did not know how they could stop at motels and rest and things like this, and she had a heart attack and died in Needles, California. It was the kind of thing that happened to our people, afraid to go in, afraid to be insulted, afraid they'll say you can't have that water or food. So they tried to drive, just stopping to rest a little bit. George and Mamie were the kindest people in the world. Of course, the last book, *A Gathering of Old Men*, was to Mr. Walter Zeno ["Pete"], who was sort of like Mathu in the book—the old man I used to speak to all the time.

MG: Do you see anything at all of value to the writer in what the critic does?

GAINES: I don't see how the critics help my writing. I think sometimes critics can bring out things in a writer's writing that he does not see. When he's writing, he always writes from the whole. I've always said He created the heavens and the earth, but why in the world did God create mosquitoes? Why in the world did God create mosquitoes and a certain state that starts with an *M*? I don't want to mention the name of the state now. But why were these things created? And God says, well, it fits into the universe in some way; everything fits. Critics can pick out things [a writer does not see]. I don't think God's going to change the things that He's created, but I think writers may look at these things—maybe they do.

I've never tried to do what the critics are saying. Well, if my agent, Dorothea, suggested I change things before the work was completed, maybe then I would have changed things around, and I did, quite often. Although we used to fight, she was probably 80 percent right. I'd argue with her, but she was 80 to 85 percent right, especially when she dealt with technical things. But that was before it was published. After it's published, it doesn't make any difference to me what people say. I can't change that around and say I'm going to something new, and I hope, something different. I don't know how those comments, those criticisms can affect a new work. I can pay closer attention to certain things, you know. I try to improve certain things each time I write, but I don't think I do it because of the critics. I think I'm my own toughest critic.

CW: At a point late in his life, Evelyn Waugh went back and revised all of his novels. Has that idea ever tempted you?

GAINES: No, not really. I know I won't ever do it. If I were an invalid confined to a bed, and nothing else could come into my mind as far as creating new things, I may think about doing something else. For example, I was thinking of putting "A Long Day in November" into a poem, a long poem, if I knew anything about poetry, but I know nothing about poetry. Something like that. But I would never think about rewriting my books. I have such great respect for my agent, and she and I worked almost like partners on those books. I mean, I did the work, but she read everything, every word, every line, every page, everything I've ever had published, she's read those things, and read them over and over and over and over. Now that she's dead, I wouldn't dare try to do anything we did—I did—while she was alive. I wouldn't do anything like that.

MG: We know that she was extremely important to you at the beginning of your work.

GAINES: Yes. For a young writer publishing his first story in a little magazine, and an agent is interested in him, that's the high point of his life. And I got in touch with her, and she said she wanted to see everything from then on that I would write. And I said yes, of course, and everything from then on, everything I wrote in college and after, she saw it. When I got out of school, I had no money at all and she was a patron. She put up money. She was much more than just an agent. As I said, she was patron, friend. She was also editor and secretary. She'd answer letters, fill out forms, you know, *Who's Who* and whatever, wherever. She used to always get on me about doing it, and I'd say I'm not going to do it. She'd say, well, OK, she'd do it, and so she'd fill them out. She was always getting on me about answering letters, and I would answer them sometime. The rest of the time I just couldn't, so she would answer their letters.

She was against publicity people coming in and trying to make me a celebrity type. She said, "Let your work do the talking." I know a lady in San Francisco who wanted me to say witty things once a week so they could go in the paper. I can't think of a damned thing to say witty. Dorothea would say don't get caught up in that kind of stuff.

She said don't go to these writers' colonies all over the place, because then you have to sit around, and you have to drink with these people, and you have to talk about things, and you have to write about the colonies, and you have to do all these kinds of things. Stay away from those things. She said, "If you stick to your work, I'll always be there with you."

The first ten years after I got out of college, between '57 and '67, were lean years. I graduated from San Francisco State in '57, and after a year I went to Stanford, '58–'59, but those were lean years, and it was she who stuck by me and paid the rent and cooked food and all kinds of things. So she was much more than an agent. There'll never be another person like that in my life. I know that. And I'm not in the position I was in at that time, because I'm not this beginner who needs this encouragement and someone to stand beside you when everything is falling apart and you don't have anyone else in the world to turn to. She was there. I needed a person like that at the time.

MG: And even from reading just that first story, she saw what you could become.

GAINES: Oh, yes, I think she did. I think she was one of the first to see it. She was the one who pushed everything. She was the one who saw "The Sky Is Gray" in the beginning, and she knew it was going to be a great story. She knew there was a great story and people were going to have to see it one day, and this was in—well, I wrote "The Sky Is Gray" in '63, published it in '64, and she just knew it. She knew from the beginning that I had the talent to do it, and I just had to discipline myself and get down and do the work. And she said, "As long as you do it, I'll be there."

MG: Was she a native of the United States, or did she immigrate?

GAINES: She came from Berlin during the Hitler years. She was sixty-seven when she died. Dorothea came from a very wealthy background. She lived in Germany, but she went to private school in England, and then when she came here as a teenager, she went to Radcliffe. She knew literature. Dorothea was not just looking at a black writer writing a black story. She knew what literature was about. She had done a lot of editorial work. She knew music. She knew the arts. She knew all the great painters' work. She taught me all these things about listening to the great artists, listening to Bach, listening to Bee-thoven, listening to Wagner, listening to these people. OK, here's Goethe's *Faust*: read that and listen to the opera. She knew all these things. She knew the great writers in Germany, and she would talk about them. She traveled a lot. And she knew all the people in New York. She had worked in a publishing house. Before she became an agent, she had been an editor. She knew literature and saw what I could do. She saw what Larry McMurtry could do, and others.

MG: What were some of the things you and she disagreed about?

GAINES: Well, I'll give you two simple ones, and then we can get off of this. For example, she could not understand when I [wrote about how] people would park cars on lawns. I'd tell her, well, you do, here. She'd say, "But it would ruin the grass," and I'd say, "Not this grass we have." I'd say that St. Augustine grass we have around here is not going to be ruined by it. Little things like that, those kinds of disagreements. Another one was that, in one of the drafts of *A Gathering of Old Men*, I had when Gil and Sully come to Fix's house, before Fix would talk to Gil, he would make them eat. Gil and Sully went into the kitchen to eat—they had étouffée and all that sort of thing—and there was beer. Dorothea said Cajuns are French and Frenchmen drink wine. I said, Dorothea, Cajuns down here drink beer. Maybe in France a lot of people drink wine, but these Cajuns down here drink beer, and I know that. "Well, no, I cannot agree with you, E. I cannot agree with you. If they're French, they drink wine with their food." I said I won't change this because I know they'd drink beer. We'd argue about these little things.

But there were bigger things. For example, in the original draft of *Catherine Carmier*, there was sort of a love interest between Jack-son and Lillian, rather than Catherine. I mean, I wrote that book so many times, hell, everybody was in love with somebody. So there were these two people coming in, these two lost people, and they were both trying to find a place in the world to rest, like those birds [a mocking-bird in a bush immediately outside the window of the sun porch on which we are sitting is singing loudly; the bird's voice is distinct on the tape] trying to find a little limb to rest on, and where are they going to rest in peace? Dorothea was completely against Lillian. She said: "No, Lillian is crazy. If Jackson wants someone, it could not be Lillian because Lillian is lost, and where would two lost people go?" I said: "I don't know. Maybe that's why they're attracted to each other." She said, "No!" And I thought about that for two or three years before I saw Catherine as that central person. Then I realized how right she was, that Catherine would be the person who would be in the background and sort of watching him all the time, because wherever Lillian and Jackson were together, Catherine was always around.

MG: What was the original title?

GAINES: Oh, I called it "A Little Stream," and at one time I called it "Barren Summer." As a matter of fact, some people have mentioned that my first novel was *Barren Summer* and my second novel was *Catherine Carmier*. I rewrote that book so many times that by the time I sent it back to New York, I just had "Catherine," and the editor there said we needed something more than just "Catherine." I said I don't know what else to call it. So finally I said, call it *Catherine Carmier*; just put a last name on it. So he said OK. But I wish now that I had stuck to the title "Barren Summer," because it's a barren summer for them all. Nobody gets anything out of that summer. Anyway, Dorothea was much against that Lillian-Jackson relationship, just vehemently against it. It took me quite a while.

But I disagreed with Malcolm Cowley on things like that, too. Then, years later, I would agree with him. It's like I've told my students here, "OK, you can disagree with me here now, but twenty-five years later, you're going to knock on my door and say, 'You're right.' I know damned well you're going to knock on my door and say it."

MG: Where did you know Malcolm Cowley?

GAINES: At Stanford. Another thing I remember is, I couldn't think of a title for "The Sky Is Gray." I was trying to think of titles, and I called it "A Little Southern Town" because I'd been listening to a lot of Charlie Parker and Charlie Parker had this tune called "A Little Spanish Town." So I said, "A Little Southern Town," and Dorothea said, "That is a lousy title!" I said OK, we'll think of something else. And once I said "The Sky Is Gray," she said, oh yeah, that's OK. We'd work on titles together. We'd do all kinds of things together.

Miss Jane was "A Short Biography of Miss Jane Pittman," and I just changed it to *The Autobiography* without any help there. *Of Love and Dust* came natural. The original title of *A Gathering of Old Men* was "The Revenge of Old Men," but I changed that around because these guys don't get any revenge; they're just gathering.

CW: What about *In My Father's House?*

GAINES: Oh, yes, that's a good one. I wanted one of those Greek tragic titles. I wanted to write something, and it was called "Revenge at St. Adrian"—that's the town it takes place in. I think we argued about that, too. Oh, yeah, we had arguments about the different things. I was going Greek tragedy all the way, everybody killing off everybody. I forget exactly who got killed, I wrote that story so many times. I remember Dorothea disagreeing with me on lots of points in it. I realized later how right she was. She was right more than anyone else I've ever dealt with.

MG: But usually right on technical things. The things she seems not to have been right on were when she tried to get you to change something that had to do with the culture in South Louisiana.

GAINES: Yes, but she was right on the Lillian-Catherine thing. That was not technical; that was philosophical. She was right there. She was right in many of the characters of *A Gathering of Old Men*. The thing I had the most difficulty with, she was right about.

CW: What was that?

GAINES: *Catherine Carmier* and *In My Father's House*, the omniscient-point-of-view books. She was always right there, because I had more problems with those two books than all the other books put together.

Now, I don't know whether she was right or wrong in "Just Like a Tree." I remember writing "Just Like a Tree," and she loved that story. That's one of her favorite ones in the *Bloodline* stories—that book is dedicated to her, too. I had a little funny story within the story. You know, it's told by different characters, and one of the characters in the story—the character I based on my brother Lionel—tells a funny story that will make people laugh. Because everybody's going to hang around the place [Aunt Fe's house] and they're sort of gloomy. It's a funny story about a preacher who's going to try to prove he can walk on water, and he falls down. He has these boards just underneath the water, and he's walking out there and somebody—he has three boards going out there in that river—and somebody removed that middle board. He's going to walk from the bank out there, and his deacons are keeping the people back so they can't see those boards. So he's going to walk out there on that water, and I think it's one of the funniest things I've ever written.

This young kid would tell this story in "Just Like a Tree" and make people laugh. It's mentioned in there. It's mentioned a guy just told a funny story. That's when the white woman comes in there, and she hears people laughing. You don't get the story, but she says, "These niggers can laugh even if someone was beaten to death." She didn't understand why the story was told. The story is not told in the book— I had to take it out—but this is the story she heard when she came walking up to the place. So I sent this thing to Andrew Lytle, and Lytle says, "I just love the story, but *that* has to come out because it slows down the progress of the story." Dorothea almost went crazy: "No!" I said, "Listen, D. O., this guy's going to pay me 350, 375 dollars. I guess I have to take this out of there."

MG: So she wanted it to stay in.

GAINES: Oh, yes, because it's so funny. I loved it. I loved it. But Lytle's the editor. And sometimes I'd go over her head, but very, very seldom that I ever did.

CW: You didn't put it back in when you put it in the book.

GAINES: Oh, no. I think after a while she began to see that it was better. But it was so good that she wanted it—and I wanted it—and I asked Lytle do I have to take it, and he said, yeah, take it out.

MG: You could put it in somewhere else.

GAINES: Yeah, the old story about Picasso and the sun. Picasso painted this beautiful picture, and he had the sun in it. Someone stood there watching Picasso paint it, and the guy goes back the next day, and the sun is no longer there. He says, "Pablo, what happened to the sun, such a beautiful sun?" And Picasso said: "It doesn't fit. I took it out, and I'll put it in another place." So you just put these kinds of things in someplace else. Maybe not in that same form, but you put it someplace else. I think I might have put it in *Miss Jane Pittman* in some kind of comic way or put it in *A Gathering of Old Men* in some kind of comic way.

Another thing Dorothea wanted me to do, she wanted me to leave Dial after *Miss Jane*. She wanted me to leave Dial before *Miss Jane Pittman*, and she thought that Dial did not do enough to promote the *Bloodline* stories, and she felt that we ought to get away from Dial. I argued with her there. I said, "No, Dial gave me a break when nobody else was interested in my work." I said Dial came through and gave me a break. And I said I would give them that novel. She wanted me to go to a bigger publishing house that would really promote that novel, and she always felt that if we had gone with *Miss Jane* to a bigger name—Knopf or Random House—I would have gotten the kind of publicity she felt I deserved to have. So she was always looking out for my interests. Not for money's sake. I mean, she needed money, she wanted money, too, but she would never push a piece of work that she did not think was worth her time. But we had disagreements over things.

CW: Your publishers: Atheneum, Dial, and Knopf, is that right?

GAINES: Yeah. Atheneum did *Catherine Carmier*, but after that, Dorothea and Hiram Haydn didn't get along too well, so we went to the Dial Press.

CW: And you stayed with them through *Of Love and Dust*, *Bloodline*, and *Miss Jane*.

GAINES: And the little story, *A Long Day in November* [the children's-book version].

CW: Then why did you finally leave them?

GAINES: Dorothea always wanted to leave. She felt they should've done more for *Bloodline*, and when they didn't really push *Miss Jane*, she said, "We've got to get away from these people." And then we went to Knopf.

MG: How do you feel about how Knopf has handled *A Gathering of Old Men*?

GAINES: Well, I never get in and try to promote these things myself. Dorothea always felt that they never did do enough, and I can only go along with her. But I don't know. I'm not a best-seller. These people put these big ads behind the Mailers, whose books are going to sell hundreds of thousands of copies, and sell it to paperback for a million dollars, or two or three million dollars. I'll never sell a book for a million dollars. Hell, if I get forty thousand or fifty thousand dollars, they think that I have a gun in their face.

MG: It's obvious that you decided somewhere along the way that you were going to write literature that you felt was worthy of the name, that your novels were going to be good writing, that you would not simply write books to make money. Do you think Dorothea influenced you in that?

GAINES: Oh, no. I probably would have tried to write these. I think the basic thing I would have put in my books, but I think I would have done a lot of other things that should have been edited out of the books. Which she made me do. Well, I mean, she *suggested* that I do, and in no small terms: "Get this shit out of this book." And she'd always come back with, "E., you write so much better than this." And that's the thing that really gets to you: "Oh, boy, now she's going to use that." So she'd go to your best thing, she'd go back to the best thing you've written, and say, "Now look at how beautiful this is, oh, look at this."

All right. Now, the basic thing, she didn't tell me to go out and write literature. I knew what I wanted to write about. But it was she who would say, "OK, I think this whole passage here, you're doing that for effect. Don't do that. Get that out of there." Sometime I couldn't see the forest for the trees. Sometime I'd put a lot of things in there, and I did not know I was going the wrong way. Probably a year or so later, I would have seen it. These are the kinds of things she saw as soon as she saw the manuscript. If my books have been called a success as "literature," it was because I had her. She did a lot to help me to clean up the thing.

MG: That's another thing for students, that you don't write a masterpiece quickly. You don't just whip one off.

GAINES: Well, I'd hate for students to think that someone else is going to write their books for them. Nobody else is going to write your books. Your editor can't write the book, your agent can't write the book, your teacher can't write your book. You must write your own book. I think all major writers have had someone to bounce this material off of. Shakespeare even had to work things out on stage. I'm pretty sure "To be or not to be" didn't work out in just one time. I'm pretty sure he had to do that over and over and over.

CW: That's what rehearsals are for.

GAINES: That's what rehearsals are for! Cut that stuff out of there. This stuff isn't working right, get that out of there. Beethoven's writing da-da-da-daa, and there's a story about one time Beethoven's old lady says, "Look, Ludwig, what're you doing with all this da-da-da-daa stuff?" and that's how he got the idea. I'm thinking about someone as great as Tolstoy reading his material to people around him and asking, "What do you think of that?" He knew he was the greatest, but he just wanted to see what you think. And people would answer, "Yes, Count, that's great," and he'd say, "Without false modesty, much like the *Iliad*, huh?" You know, Hemingway and Gertrude Stein—and, you know, Faulkner had a friend there in Oxford, Phil Stone, and Sherwood Anderson in New Orleans—and they'd talk about literature. And of course, where would Faulkner be today, if old Malcolm Cowley had not come through in '46 for him? Faulkner was as dead in '45, '46 as anyone could be dead, and Cowley came along and wrote this thing, and all the others recognized Faulkner as the great genius of the twentieth century. He was the genius of the twentieth century before Cowley did it, and while Sartre and certain critics were aware of it, the people were not aware of it.

MG: That's one of the roles of the critic: when people don't realize the importance of a writer's work, or understand it, he opens it up to them.

GAINES: Oh, yes, opening it up to the reader, but I don't know what Cowley did to help the writer. I remember Cowley suggesting to Faulkner—Cowley said to me—about "The Bear," that it would be perfect if he got a certain part of it out of there. I think it's a flashback scene, but I don't remember what part it is. And he also told Faulkner that parts of *Absalom, Absalom!* should be cut out completely. Of course, Faulkner had already written that stuff, and Faulkner's not going back just because Cowley said cut that out.

MG: It seems it's the agent and the editor who are of value to the writer. The critic is really more of value to the reader.

GAINES: That's why one of the books I recommend for my students is that biography of Max Perkins by [Scott A.] Berg. I mean, when you realize that Perkins was the editor of Hemingway, Fitzgerald, and Wolfe, and so many other writers of the twentieth century—and this man had to work. This man was these guys' father. They needed him.

CW: Hiram Haydn was your editor at Atheneum?

GAINES: Yes.

CW: Doctorow was your editor at Dial?

GAINES: Ed was the editor-in-chief. Bill Decker was my editor at Dial. My first editor at Knopf was Robert Gottlieb, who has left now and is editor of the *New Yorker*, and Ash Green is my editor at Knopf now.

CW: What kinds of differences are there in the working relationships you've had with those various editors?

GAINES: Dorothea knew Hiram Haydn, and I think, mostly, information went through her, and then Dorothea would send it on to me. Bill and I had a good relationship at Dial. Bill had formerly been a Stanfordite. Bill was a former cowboy, and he knew the outdoors and told great stories. I like people who can tell great stories, and he's a great storyteller and knows how to relax and eat well and drink well. He could sit around and discuss a piece of work, not from an "editor's" point of view, but like almost from a friend's point of view. For example, a year before I changed *The Autobiography of Miss Jane Pittman*, Bill said, "I think that book should be told from that old lady's point of view." I said, "I don't know, man." It took me a year to realize it. So I had that kind of relationship with Bill, a guy who could just sit around and talk, spend hours with him. Gottlieb and I were not very close. Gottlieb let you know when you came into the room that he was a genius, so I said, "Well, OK."

MG: It's hard to talk to geniuses.

GAINES: And he was dealing with a book that was very difficult for me, and he was trying to tell me how to write it.

CW: He did *In My Father's House*, didn't he?

GAINES: Yes, and it was a very difficult book for me, and he was trying to tell me how to improve it. I disagreed with him, and he could see that it was not going to be any kind of big thing, and he just let me know that he knew what he was talking about. Then after that book was not a successful book—it was the least successful of all my books—I don't think he had any further interest, and since Dorothea was going to keep me at Knopf, that's when Ash Green just came in, and Ash and I get along quite well.

MG: Is there one form, the short story or the novel, that you feel is more your form than the other?

GAINES: I think I would feel more comfortable with the novella form. The novel takes a long time, and the short story is—well, as Faulkner once said, a well-written short story is much like writing poetry. You have to really work at it. I think one of the reasons that I have not written more short stories is I cannot think of any more stories to write. I think the novella length would be the length for my talent. My novels are not very big. My novels are two hundred, three hundred pages.

CW: When you say novella, what are you thinking of in manuscript pages?

GAINES: I'm saying 125 to 150 pages to print 80 to 100 pages, something like that. I did "A Long Day in November," but I don't know if I can ever do anything else of that length. But my novels are short novels, and I know I will never be able to write a big one, a thousand-page thing.

CW: You don't see a *War and Peace* coming out.

GAINES: I had one idea, but I know I won't do it now. There is a *War and Peace* out there, and I've talked about it before. I've called it "Decade," and that would be the decade between '58 and '68, beginning with the march from Selma to Montgomery, then the death of King in '68. During those ten years things were happening in this country where you drew your participants from the poorest, most illiterate person in the fields to the president and the attorney general of the United States, and all these people participating in the same cause at that time. You had your war veterans and you had poor whites and you had poor blacks, and you had this great man, King, and you had all these great workers, and you had all this violence—all this—and I think that can produce as great a novel as anything we've ever done.

But you have to have the time to do it. And as someone said

about *Miss Jane Pittman*, you have to sift out the stuff that is not necessary, just bring in the stuff that is—because we had enough things going on there. We had the big families whom you can use, as Tolstoy does in *War and Peace* and *Anna Karenina*. You have those big families from different parts of the country and how they contributed and who their children are and who their grandchildren are, and how Hollywood and New York and Washington worked together—all these things—it's all there. But you need someone at least with my ear for dialogue to bring it off. I'm being facetious. I know I can't do it, because I think it would take me ten to twelve years to do it.

MG: It's not the talent but the time!

GAINES: Oh, yes, it's time—the time and the energy and not having anything to do with classes or anything. Sit out on that boat and do this when you want to do it, and have twenty students doing research for you and bring this stuff all to you, and have, you know, a good buddy, and you sit down and start with this pile of papers and sort this stuff out. It would need a lot of work, and I couldn't do all the footwork myself. I could never do the footwork that's necessary. I could never read enough books all by myself.

You get one of these young fellows out there, twenty, thirty years old, I would like to be his mentor on something like this. If a kid from USL came up to me and said, "Dr. Gaines, I'd like to try that," I'd say: "Okay, you write me a hundred-page story or novella and let me see how well you can work. I want to see if you have narrative form. I want to see if you have dialogue together. I want to see if you have research together. I want to see if you can develop characters." And then I'll say to the USL administrators, I want to work with this student here for a living, until he writes this book. And I'm going to nail him in that damned room until he writes this book. If I came across a student like that, I'd work with him. I'd spend most of my time with him. I wouldn't write. I wouldn't do anything—if I saw a student who really meant it and who had the talent.

MG: You wouldn't want to encourage mediocre talent.

GAINES: Well, it's that I would feel there are lots of people out there I could give some help to. Why give all my help to some guy over here who's not going to bring this off? But if he looks like somebody I know has the talent to bring it off, and if he looks like he has the discipline—oh, he'd have to have discipline, because we'd lock him up and I'd say: "OK, we know you have talent. Now when you write me twenty, fifty pages, I'll let you out of that room. I'm just going to throw your food in there, and when you write me twenty, fifty pages, then you can come out, come out and run around Girard Park awhile and get your exercise, and get back in there."

MG: Was that the kind of mentor Dorothea was?

GAINES: Oh, no, she would never do that. She would always want to know, "Did you do your exercise today?" Dorothea believed in keeping up your physical body along with the mental body. "How much reading did you do? How much drinking?" No matter what I said—if I told her two she knew I'd had four. If I told her one, she knew it was three. She'd say, "E., lay off that drinking." She would always ask what did you write and how was it going. She understood when I would write a week and didn't produce anything. I would tell her. She'd say, "How did it come out?" and I would say, "Nothing." She'd say, "Just start again on Monday."

She knew that. She knew so much about literature that she knew you couldn't work all the time. One of the last things she told me was, "Don't rush, don't push yourself on these things." She always felt that if you were a real writer—and she always knew that I was—when it comes, you're going to put it down, and you can't rush it. You can't rush these things, but when it's there, don't avoid it. Don't be running after this woman or that woman, or getting so damned drunk you can't do your work, or having a good time here so you can't do your work. If it's there, do your work. She knew that I would. She was against my teaching for a long time because she always felt that teaching would take it away. And in a way it does. Both she and I agreed, years ago when I was offered teaching jobs all over the place, that I didn't want a continuing job. I would go out for a couple of weeks or a month or so and get on back to work.

CW: You've told us before about how you had to work at the insurance company to make a living and how you locked yourself in the washroom to write on paper towels. How long have you been not working outside other than the occasional teaching situation? How long have you been free to concentrate just on your writing?

GAINES: And teaching? You know, you say you've been writing for the last twenty years, and people say, "But have you had a job?" I haven't had a job since '66.

MG: What were you doing?

GAINES: I was working as a printer's helper. I was working in this print shop. Dorothea found me the job, too. I was setting type. I'd take these little tweezers, and piece by piece by piece, I was setting those durned things. This guy used to print up a lot of cards and posters and letters, and I knew all about types and sizes, the different shapes of them. I used to love to do it. I did that for about three years, I guess. I know I was doing it in '66. I must have started in '63, '64.

MG: How did Dorothea feel about your coming to Louisiana to teach?

GAINES: Well, she wasn't particularly crazy about it, and neither was I in the beginning, in '81. She thought they would have too much control over me here. And she didn't want that. No, she was against it because, she said: "After that, then they want to control your life, and I've fought so hard for you to be free! And no one can control your life. You just do your work."

MG: Did she change her mind?

GAINES: Oh, I think when she understood what kind of relationship I had down here, she was all right. After *In My Father's House*, I was in desperate need of some form of security. That book made no money, and not too long after that I broke my leg and had all kinds of problems, so I was in desperate need of some kind of security. I felt I needed not to run all over this country anymore, but to settle down. But it was only after I had been given tenure here—and the house—that I said, "This is OK." I was tired moving all over the country, and I planned to come here to stay. I had not planned to come here at this time. If someone had said, say seven or eight years from now, when you're sixty, would you come, I would have said, oh, yeah, sure. But not at that particular time. But when everything was offered to me, then I just accepted it. She wasn't crazy about it, but I told her that I thought everything would work out all right.

CW: Obviously she had a change of heart, because when I saw her in New York [April, 1984], she told me how much she really appreciated how this had worked out.

MG: Do you ever regret making the decision to come to USL?

GAINES: Oh, no, no, no. No way, not by a long shot. I could not think of any other place. If LSU offered me something at about the same time, I probably would have gone to LSU. But now I would not go to LSU or any other place. I would not give up the situation as I have it now even for a place in California. Now, there could come a time when certain kinds of things could happen or certain pressures could be put on me. Anything can happen to cause friction within the administration or problems with the place where I live. But as things are now, I just cannot see myself giving up my position here, my place here, for any other place in the country.

8
Looking Ahead

CW: In looking over the range of all your work, what areas are you least satisfied with in terms of the goals you set for yourself as a writer and continue to set for yourself as a writer?

GAINES: I never set goals. I never say I'm going to write ten books or twelve books. I just say I will write as long as I know how.

CW: Not quantitatively, but qualitatively.

GAINES: Well, I just try to write better every day.

CW: Are there things you wanted to do in terms of technique, or style, or subject matter, or theme, or whatever that you wanted to do?

GAINES: I think that in every book I can develop something more. I think I'd write *Catherine Carmier* a larger book. As a matter of fact, I tried to do that until Wallace Stegner and several others told me to cut it down because—Malcolm Cowley as well—the action of the book was not moving, with all the things I wanted to include. I wanted people sitting around and eating gumbo and talking and shelling peas and making quilts and building moss mattresses—I wanted to do all that sort of thing. They said this is not moving the story. This is telling something about Louisiana rural life, but the story's not being moved. I wouldn't dare think about doing it, but if I had to write *Catherine Carmier* all over again, these are the kinds of things that I would bring into the story. I would try to show these old Creoles as I knew them as a child. That is lacking there. And *Of Love and Dust*, I really don't know what I'd do with that. It's a fun reading story, and I don't know what I'd do with it. I can do a lot with *The Autobiography of Miss Jane Pittman*. I could bring in much more of the folk stuff.

CW: Is there anything that you can think of in terms of style, technique, or form you would like to try that you haven't tried?

GAINES: I never know, because the project determines how the work should be done. For example, *Catherine Carmier* was told from the multiple point of view at one time. It just didn't work. Hell, I had people telling this thing that were getting killed. It wasn't working. There were no quarters, as a matter fact, in the first draft. They lived back in the fields, where there was a stream of water, and I had once called the book "The Little Stream" because that was the small body of water that separated them. So, I tried to write it from that multiple point of view, but it just didn't work. The book had to be a small book because of the influence of Turgenev's *Fathers and Sons* at that time. And it had to be set up the way Turgenev's book is set up. I couldn't bring in that multiple point of view, and I couldn't bring in all these old people shelling peas and making mattresses and making quilts, either, because it isn't like that in *Fathers and Sons*. Bazarov comes to this place. He must be there with the old for a while, he falls in love, and he must die. Jackson's the same way. He comes there for a little while with the old people, he falls in love, and he must leave. So you couldn't bring in all the other things. That's what dictated why the story was told that way. I didn't know any other way to tell it. I could tell [that writing] from Catherine's point of view wasn't going to work. It damned sure wouldn't work from Lillian's point of view. Jackson couldn't tell it. Brother maybe could have, but I don't know if he could have told Raoul's side. You have all these things. So you just keep working and working until you get it.

MG: Students always ask—because there are similarities between you and Jackson—to what extent is this autobiographical?

GAINES: No, there was no Catherine for me when I came back.

CW: How old were you when you first came back?

GAINES: About seventeen. I came back two years after I left. I left in '48, came back in '50. Auntie died in '53. I didn't come back then. I couldn't; I didn't have any money. After that I came back in '58. So I came back in '50, which was two years after I had gone, then in '58, which was ten years after I had gone.

CW: If there was no Catherine, were there any expectations on anyone's part that you might come back and stay?

GAINES: No. As I said, my aunt had already died, and there was no one else here.

MG: Your grandmother wasn't here?

GAINES: I wasn't that close to my grandmother, that she expected me to do things like that. They didn't expect that of me.

MG: When you left here, did you intend that one day you'd come back?

GAINES: No way! I knew I'd always come back to my aunt, but no way to stay. I didn't know when I was leaving how close I would be to her. I knew how much I loved her then, but I didn't know that thirty-nine years later I would still feel a very closeness to her and to the land—I mean to her and to our patch of land. I don't want people to think I'm so desperately in love with Louisiana or the South, as much as I am with that postage stamp in that area. That's the thing that I'm talking about.

MG: It seems that it's not so much an attachment to the land as it is an attachment to those people.

GAINES: Well, there's an attachment to both. See, if it was only the people, it would be only the living, but I'm looking after the dead now. That earth where they've rotted back there, you know, to dust again. That's what I was trying to do in *A Gathering of Old Men*, where these graves have not been kept up, and they've all sunken in, and they've all mixed again, getting back to the dirt again. The dirt is there, and they're all mixed up there, just as they used to mix up the jambalaya and the gumbo when they were alive. They're mixed up again down there.

CW: A couple of weeks ago you said your life is not as calm as most people seem to think it is. What causes you the most continuing unrest?

GAINES: Reagan.

MG: Reagan?

GAINES: People who build bombs and might use them one day.

CW: What causes you the kind of continuing unrest that has something to do with your work as an artist, as a writer?

GAINES: I don't have time to work anymore.

CW: You may have to get very selfish with your time.

GAINES: I have to do it, because if I don't, I won't get any work done. I'll never write again.

MG: What about your work in progress? Can you tell us anything about it?

GAINES: I can say that it deals with a teacher who visits a guy on death row. That has been said in the opening chapter, when the defense is trying to get something less than the death penalty for him.

This guy is going into a bar. He's as broke as anything. He doesn't have any money, and he's going into this bar, and it's probably cold weather like this. Two guys come along and say, hey, man, do you want a ride? He says, all right. So he gets into the car with them, and these guys don't have any money. And he says, I don't have a penny on me. These guys start talking about how we need a bottle, want some booze. Let's go over to the old man. We've spent our money there all the time, and he should be able to let us have a pint until grinding, until the sugarcane-cutting time.

When they go into the store, the old man's there all by himself, and this guy, this third guy, goes along in that store with them. The old man knows them and speaks to them the way he does all the time, saying hello and how's your family and all that kind of stuff. One of them speaks to him and he says, we want a bottle of wine. The old man says, OK, give me your money. When they put the money on the counter, he knows there's not enough money. He says, no, no, no, you bring your money, then you'll get your bottle. They say, come on, you know we're good for it. The old man says, no, no, so one of the guys starts going around the counter. He's going to take it. The old man says, hey, don't come back here. I told you already, you must bring the money. The guy is walking toward him, so the old man breaks toward his cash register where he has a gun.

This guy standing back doesn't know what the hell is going on around him. All of a sudden, there is shooting all around. When he realizes what has happened, the old man is dying, and these two guys are dead. And then he doesn't know what to do. He hears this voice calling him and calling him, and he doesn't know what to do. Finally he goes around the counter. The old man is dying, and the guy feels, "God, he knows I was here and now he's going to blame me for all this. He's going to tell."

He doesn't know what he's doing. He just grabs a bottle and he starts drinking. He's looking at this man and drinking and drinking and drinking like this. And as he turns he sees the cash register is open from when the old man grabbed the revolver, and he grabs the money. He says, "I need money." By now the old man has died.

This is told from a teacher's point of view—who knows nothing about any of this. I get all of this later. As he starts out, two men come into the place. Now, you see this kind of action during the trial. This happens in the forties. That's why I wanted to see the local prisons where the executions went on at that time. The trial goes on. The jury is made up of twelve white men, and this kid is sentenced to death, although he says he had nothing to do with it. But the prosecutor says, wait awhile. He went there with those guys. He's telling us he had nothing to do with it. We don't know that. We know that everybody's dead except him, and he came out of the place with a bottle and money in his pocket.

So [this] convinces the jury, and he's sentenced to die. The court-appointed defense attorney tries to get him off by saying this is not a man. This is a fool. You wouldn't call him a man. This boy has no idea what size his clothes are. He doesn't know Christmas from Fourth of July. He doesn't know a thing about Keats. He doesn't know Byron or the Bill of Rights. He can't plan any murder or robbery. He didn't do any of this. Finally he says, I'd just as soon tie down some kind of animal in the electric chair, a hog or something like that. Nevertheless, he's sentenced to die for this crime.

Now, his grandmother, or his *nanane*, or his auntie, or whoever she is, approaches this schoolteacher. She tells him: "I don't know how much time he has left—I don't know whether it's a year, several months, several weeks. Whatever, I want you to approach him and bring him to the level of a man. Then let him die as a man. That's what I want."

And this is where I am now. This teacher is sort of like I am. I don't want to have a damned thing to do with any of this. That's what he's saying at first. I don't want to have anything to do with this. The crime is there. It's over with. He's a schoolteacher on this plantation. He says, my job is to keep other kids from going that way. I want nothing with any of this. So this is what the story is about. I've reached the point now, chapter 6, that he's deciding whether or not he will go to the courthouse to visit this guy.

I still don't know what the hell he's going to say. I have no idea what he's going to say to this guy. I have no idea what the guy is going to say to him. I have no idea what the guard's going to say. I know he has a little car, a '46 Ford he drives around. I don't know where he's going to get gas from, where he's going to fill the tank. I've no idea of anything—nothing. But as the thing will move along, it will come out.

These are the problems I'm having with this. And this is what I wanted to see, what a jail looks like, how does this guy sleep. Those are small details. I have a twofold problem here. Number one, I can create the jail. That's easy for me to do. But to get that character to tell that damned story in a way that makes it flow smoothly—I don't know what the teacher wants, you see. I know the teacher doesn't want to be there, but I know damned well he's going to be there. This is the kind of conflict I'm having there. I have to get that personality together and make him do what I want him to do without controlling him. Like winding him up and saying, goddamn it, you ought to give these people the information. These people are out there waiting for you to give him that information now. I'm not going to gee-haw on you every time I want you to go left or right. You've got to do what I want you to do for me. And I haven't got him there, but I've got him to a certain point where he's doing some of the things. I haven't got him to the point where he's going to do most of it. I think I've got a pretty good start. I was working on that today. Anyway, that's what this story is about. I think it's going to be very good once I get it. I can tell it better than I can write it now, because I've been trying to write it for the last couple of years or so.

CW: How old is the boy?

GAINES: About twenty-one. He's as illiterate as someone can be. I want him on that level—not an idiot: he knows how to work, he knows how to follow orders. The defense attorney says, now, listen, he can plow, he can load sacks and pick cotton and all that sort of stuff. But we're talking about what is a man. What is a man? And this is one of the things that the teacher must find out. The teacher must say, OK, what is a man? And another conflict is in the question, why should we make this man a man if he's going to die tomorrow? Why do this? The old lady says, I want it done. The sheriff's against it because all you can do is aggravate things. Let it go. But I've got to create something that happens in the past. The little old lady says, I want it done, and your wife owes me something.

I don't know what she has on the guy's wife. These are the little tricks. I said something about tricks earlier. I must find some reason to convince that sheriff through this old lady and the sheriff's wife that the teacher will come to that jail twice a week. That's what I call little tricks. You pull all these little deals, and you throw them all in there. It's just like making gumbo. If you mix it well, you don't notice the tricks.

MG: We don't want you to tell us, but do you know whether or not he's going to be executed?

GAINES: I don't know. But I know one thing: I'm going to have him give a very good speech before it happens, if it happens. He has to stand up as a strong man and give this talk. It's almost like in *The Confessions of Nat Turner*, that there's a guy who is interested in what this guy has to say because he's followed this whole thing. It's a Pygmalion type thing, the Elephant Man type thing. I want all of that. The Helen Keller thing, you know. And there's a guy who's been following this. I don't know who this guy's going to be, whether he's going to be a newspaper guy or his defense attorney or someone else, but he's going to be there. He's going to follow everything that's going down, and he's going to make notes. The day before this guy's supposed to be executed, if the guy will be executed or not—I really don't know, to be honest with you—this guy's going to talk to him. He's going to say, tell me things, tell me what it is. And the guy's going to tell him—he's going to stand up real tall—and tell him what he thinks manliness is and citizenship and what life is about, and then he's just going to say, OK, let them do what they want.

This teacher, who is cynical—I mean, he hates teaching—says, "I hate the whole goddamned thing." Hearing what he has done for this man who was condemned will bring something out of him. And he will go back to these kids, these small kids he has around him, and he will realize he has a duty to perform. And that duty is not to run away to the North as he wanted to, to get the hell away from all of these things. But, OK, I'll just give my life here, and this is it. But this other person, this condemned man, must be the one to convert him to this, to give his life. That's what the whole thing is about. He in one way makes the condemned boy, who is like an animal, a man, and the condemned one makes *him* a man, so that he can go back to develop something. That's what this is about. If I ever get it done.

Index